**TEACHER'S PET PUBLICATIONS**

LITPLAN TEACHER PACK
for
The Cay
based on the book by
Theodore Taylor

Written by
Barbara M. Linde, MA Ed.

© 2004 Teacher's Pet Publications
All Rights Reserved

This Lit Plan on Theodore Taylor's *The Cay* has been brought to you by
Teacher's Pet Publications, Inc.

Copyright Teacher's Pet Publications 2004

Only the student materials in this unit plan may be reproduced. Pages such as worksheets and study guides may be reproduced for use in the purchaser's classroom. For any additional copyright questions, contact Teacher's Pet Publications, Inc.

www.tpet.com

TABLE OF CONTENTS – *The Cay*

Introduction	7
Unit Objectives	10
Reading Assignment Sheet	11
Unit Outline	12
Study Questions	15
Quiz/Study Questions (Multiple Choice)	29
Pre-Reading Vocabulary Worksheets	57
Lesson One (Introductory Lesson)	71
Nonfiction Assignment Sheet	75
Oral Reading Evaluation Form	77
Writing Assignment 1	81
Writing Evaluation Form	82
Writing Assignment 2	84
Extra Writing Assignments/Discussion Questions	87
Writing Assignment 3	91
Vocabulary Review Activities	95
Unit Review Activities	96
Unit Tests	103
Unit Resource Materilas	143
Vocabulary Resource Materials	167

A FEW NOTES ABOUT THE AUTHOR
THEODORE TAYLOR

TAYLOR, Theodore (1921 --) Theodore Taylor was born, in Statesville, North Carolina, near the Catawba River, on June 23, 1921. Taylor had four sisters. When he was about nine years old, he had a paper route. He delivered the papers early in the morning and then went to school.

Theodore Taylor's family moved to Norfolk, Virginia when he was a child because his father got a job at a naval yard there. When he was thirteen he got his first writing job. He worked for the *Evening Star* in Portsmouth, Virginia, writing about local high school sports. He graduated from high school, then moved to Washington, D. C. when he was seventeen. In Washington he got a job as a copyboy for the Washington, D. C. *Daily News*. He never went to college, so he learned about newspaper work from his early jobs. When he was about nineteen, he moved to New York City and got a job writing sports for NBC radio.

Taylor served in the Navy during World War II. He started out as a cadet-AB seaman on a gasoline tanker, then worked aboard four other merchant ships. He was promoted to an officer and was sent to the South Pacific. He also served in the Korean War with the Naval Reserve. His unit helped victims of hurricanes in the Caribbean Islands. This is where he got the idea for *The Cay*. He modeled Timothy and Phillip after people he met. The plot is based on a true story, and it only took Taylor about three weeks to write this book!

When he left the Navy, he went to California. His first book, called The *Magnificent Mitscher*, was published in 1955. He worked in California for Paramount Pictures for several years before starting to write full time.

The Cay won 11 awards. Taylor says he is most proud of the Lewis Carroll Shelf Award, "since the book was deemed worthy of being on a shelf with *Alice in Wonderland*." It was also named to the Horn Book honor list, the American Library Association's Notable Books, and the New York Times Best Books of the Year.

Theodore Taylor wrote many other books, including *The Maldonado Miracle*, *The Teetoncey Trilogy*, and *Sweet Friday Island*. In 1993 he wrote *Timothy of the Cay*, which is a prequel/sequel to *The Cay*. He writes for both young adults and adults, and has written novels, short stores, and novelettes.

Taylor lives with his wife in Laguna Beach, California.

For more information about Theodore Taylor, visit his Web site at www.theodoretaylor.com.

INTRODUCTION

This unit has been designed to develop students' reading, writing, thinking, listening and speaking skills through exercises and activities related to *The Cay* by Theodore Taylor. It includes 000 lessons, supported by extra resource materials.

The **introductory lesson** introduces students to *The Cay*. Following the introductory activity, students are given an explanation of how the activity relates to the book they are about to read. Following the transition, students are given the materials they will be using during the unit. At the end of the lesson, students begin the pre-reading work for the first reading assignment.

The **reading assignments** are approximately 30 pages each; some are a little shorter while others are a little longer. Students have approximately 15 minutes of pre-reading work to do prior to each reading assignment. This pre-reading work involves reviewing the study questions for the assignment and doing some vocabulary work for 8 to 10 vocabulary words they will encounter in their reading.

The **study guide questions** are fact-based questions; students can find the answers to these questions right in the text. These questions come in two formats: short answer or multiple choice. The best use of these materials is probably to use the short answer version of the questions as study guides for students (since answers will be more complete), and to use the multiple-choice version for occasional quizzes. It might be a good idea to make transparencies of your answer keys for the overhead projector.

The **vocabulary work** is intended to enrich students' vocabularies as well as to aid in the students' understanding of the book. Prior to each reading assignment, students will complete a two-part worksheet for approximately 8 to 10 vocabulary words in the upcoming reading assignment. Part I focuses on students' use of general knowledge and contextual clues by giving the sentence in which the word appears in the text. Students are then to write down what they think the words mean based on the words' usage. Part II gives students dictionary definitions of the words and has them match the words to the correct definitions based on the words' contextual usage. Students should then have an understanding of the words when they meet them in the text.

After each reading assignment, students will go back and formulate answers for the study guide questions. Discussion of these questions serves as a **review** of the most important events and ideas presented in the reading assignments.

After students complete extra discussion questions, there is a **vocabulary review** lesson which pulls together all of the separate vocabulary lists for the reading assignments and gives students a review of all of the words they have studied.

Following the reading of the book, two lessons are devoted to the **extra discussion questions/writing assignments**. These questions focus on interpretation, critical analysis and personal response, employing a variety of thinking skills and adding to the students' understanding of the novel. These questions are done as a **group activity**. Using the information they have acquired so far through individual work and class discussions, students get together to further examine the text and to brainstorm ideas relating to the themes of the novel.

The group activity is followed by a **reports and discussion** session in which the groups share their ideas about the book with the entire class; thus, the entire class gets exposed to many different ideas regarding the themes and events of the book.

There are three **writing assignments** in this unit, each with the purpose of informing, persuading, or having students express personal opinions. The first assignment is to **inform.** Students will research procedures for evacuating a sinking ship and then write directions for doing so. The second writing assignment is to **persuade**. Students will write a letter asking the government to continue searching for Phillip and Timothy. The third writing assignment is to offer a **personal opinion.** Students will offer an opinion about whether Phillip and Mrs. Enright should have stayed on Curaçao or traveled to the United States.

In addition, there is a **nonfiction reading assignment**. Students are required to read a piece of nonfiction related in some way to *The Cay*. After reading their nonfiction pieces, students will fill out a worksheet on which they answer questions regarding facts, interpretation, criticism, and personal opinions. During one class period, students make **oral presentations** about the nonfiction pieces they have read. This not only exposes all students to a wealth of information, it also gives students the opportunity to practice **public speaking**.

The **review lesson** pulls together all of the aspects of the unit. The teacher is given four or five choices of activities or games to use which all serve the same basic function of reviewing all of the information presented in the unit.

The **unit tes**t comes in two formats: all multiple choice-matching-true/false or with a mixture of matching, short answer, and composition. As a convenience, two different tests for each format have been included.

There are additional **support materials** included with this unit. The **Unit Resource Materials** section includes suggestions for an in-class library, crossword and word search puzzles related to the novel, and extra vocabulary worksheets. There is a list of **bulletin board ideas** which gives the teacher suggestions for bulletin boards to go along with this unit. In addition, there is a list of **extra class activities** the teacher could choose from to enhance the unit or as a substitution for an exercise the teacher might feel is inappropriate for his/her class. **Answer keys** are located directly after the **reproducible student materials** throughout the unit. The student materials may be reproduced for use in the purchaser's classroom without infringement of copyrights. No other portion of this unit may be reproduced without the written consent of Teacher's Pet Publications, Inc.

UNIT PLAN ADAPTATIONS

Block Schedule

Depending on the length of your class periods, and the frequency with which the class meets, you may wish to choose one of the following options:
- Complete two of the daily lessons in one class period.
- Have students complete all reading and writing activities in class.
- Assign all reading to be completed out of class, and concentrate on the worksheets and discussions in class.
- Assign the projects from Daily Lesson Fifteen at the beginning of the unit, and allow time each day for students to work on them.
- Use some of the Unit and Vocabulary Resource activities during every class.

Gifted & Talented / Advanced Classes
- Emphasize the projects and the extra discussion questions.
- Have students complete all of the writing activities.
- Assign the reading to be completed out of class and focus on the discussions in class.
- Encourage students to develop their own questions.

ESL / ELD
- Assign a partner to help the student read the text aloud.
- Tape record the text and have the student listen and follow along in the text.
- Give the student the study guide worksheets to use as they read.
- Provide pictures and demonstrations to explain difficult vocabulary words and concepts.

UNIT OBJECTIVES
The Cay

1. Through reading *The Cay students* will analyze characters and their situations to better understand the themes of the novel.

2. Students will demonstrate their understanding of the text on four levels: factual, interpretive, critical, and personal.

3. Students will practice reading aloud and silently to improve their skills in each area.

4. Students will enrich their vocabularies and improve their understanding of the novel through the vocabulary lessons prepared for use in conjunction with it.

5. Students will answer questions to demonstrate their knowledge and understanding of the main events and characters in *The Cay*.

6. Students will practice writing through a variety of writing assignments.

7. The writing assignments in this are geared to several purposes:
    a. To check the students' reading comprehension
    b. To make students think about the ideas presented by the novel
    c. To make students put those ideas into perspective
    d. To encourage critical and logical thinking
    e. To provide the opportunity to practice good grammar and improve students' use of the English language.

8. Students will read aloud, report, and participate in large and small group discussions to improve their public speaking and personal interaction skills.

READING ASSIGNMENT SHEET
The Cay

Date Assigned	Reading Assignment Chapters	Completion Date Prior to Class on This Date
	Chapters 1-2	
	Chapters 3-5	
	Chapters 6-9	
	Chapters 10-12	
	Chapters 13-15	
	Chapters 16-19	

WRITING ASSIGNMENT LOG
The Cay

Date to be Assigned	Assignment	Completion Date Prior to Class on This Date
	Writing Assignment 1	
	Writing Assignment 2	
	Writing Assignment 3	
	Non-fiction Assignment	

UNIT OUTLINE – *The Cay*

1 Introduction Distribute Unit Materials PV 1-2	2 Read 1-2 Study ?? 1-2	3 PVR 3-5 Oral Reading Evaluation	4 Quiz 1-5 PVR 6-9	5 Writing Assignment #1 Nonfiction
6 Study ?? 6-9 PVR 10-12	7 Study ?? 10-12 PVR 13-15	8 Study ?? 13-15 Writing Assignment #2	9 Writing Conference	10 PVR 16-19 Study ?? 16-19
11 Extra Discussion ??	12 Writing Assignment #3	13 Library Work	14 Audio Cassette and Discussion	15 Nonfiction Assignment
16 Vocabulary Review	17 Review	18 Test	19	20

Key: P = Preview Study Questions V = Vocabulary Work R = Read

STUDY GUIDE QUESTIONS

SHORT ANSWER STUDY GUIDE QUESTIONS - *The Cay*

Chapter 1
1. What did Phillip do that he wasn't supposed to do?
2. Identify Henrik van Boven.
3. How was the fort different on this visit than before?
4. What was different at the Queen Emma pontoon bridge?
5. Where did Phillip's father work?
6. Where were the Enrights from? What were they doing in Curacao?

Chapter 2
1. What kept Phillip awake most of the night?
2. Why did the Chinese crews on the tankers refuse to sail?
3. Identify SS *Empire Tern*.
4. What effect did the sinking of the *Tern* have on Phillip?
5. What was Phillip's reaction to his mother's telling him they were leaving the island to go home to Norfolk?
6. Phillip didn't want to leave Curacao and thought about hiding. Why didn't he hide?
7. Identify the SS *Hato*.
8. Describe the parting of Phillip and his mother from his dad.

Chapter 3
1. When was the *Hato* torpedoed?
2. How did Phillip and his mother get separated?
3. What happened to Phillip as he went into the water?
4. Describe the man Phillip saw when he came to after being hit in the head going into the water.
5. Who was on the raft with Phillip?
6. What did the Negro man call Phillip?
7. What happened to Phillip's mother?
8. Identify Stew.
9. What "rare good luck" did Phillip and Timothy have?
10. Identify Timothy.

Chapter 4
1. Where was Timothy's home?
2. Timothy told Phillip they had something very important to do the next day. What was it?
3. The pain went away from Phillip's head, but what happened that was worse?
4. What did Timothy say about Phillip's condition?
5. How did Phillip feel he realized his condition? What did he do?

Study Guide Questions *The Cay*

Chapter 5
1. What hopeful thing happened toward noon on the third day that Phillip and Timothy were on the raft?
2. What did Timothy say was bad luck?
3. What did Phillip ask Timothy to tell him? What did Timothy do?
4. What did Phillip wonder?

Chapter 6
1. What caused Phillip to fall off the raft and fall in the water with the sharks?
2. What did Timothy see that the raft was headed toward?
3. How did Timothy and Phillip feel about leaving the raft?
4. What words did Phillip use to describe Timothy?

Chapter 7
1. How did Phillip feel when Timothy left him alone on the beach to explore the island?
2. How did Timothy describe the island?
3. Where did Timothy plan to make their camp?
4. What was Timothy worried about?
5. How did they celebrate making landfall?

Chapter 8
1. How did Phillip describe the times he spent alone during the first few days on the island?
2. How old did Timothy say he was?
3. What two things did Timothy do to alert ships and planes of their location?
4. What did Phillip discover about Timothy as they worked?

Chapter 9
1. What did Timothy make from vines, and what was it for?
2. What did Timothy ask Phillip to do?
3. Describe the scene where Phillip lost his temper about weaving the mats.
4. Describe what happened after Phillip lost his temper.
5. What did Phillip ask Timothy to call him?

Study Guide Questions *The Cay*

Chapter 10
1. What happened on their seventh night on the island, and how did they feel about it?
2. Phillip asked Timothy why there were different colors of skin. What was Timothy's answer?
3. What was the problem with getting the coconuts?
4. Phillip asked Timothy how his eyes looked. What was Timothy's answer?
5. Did Phillip's appearance bother Timothy?

Chapter 11
1. What did Timothy make to help Phillip get around?
2. Timothy was trying to make Phillip more independent. Phillip did not like to think about the reason. What did he say the reason was?
3. Timothy thought something was wrong with the island. What was it?
4. What did Timothy do to try and change their luck?

Chapter 12
1. What happened to Timothy one morning in May?
2. What did Phillip do when Timothy ran into the water?
3. Why did Phillip put sea grape leaves over Timothy's body?
4. How was Timothy when he woke up?
5. How much time went by during the time of Timothy's ordeal?

Chapter 13
1. What did Timothy decide in late May?
2. How did they keep track of the days?
3. What did Timothy teach Phillip to do? Why did Timothy think Phillip should learn this?
4. How did Phillip feel about the results of Timothy's lessons?
5. What things had Timothy never thought about? What did Phillip tell him?
6. What feat did Phillip accomplish next?
7. What did Timothy tell Phillip after this success?
8. That night, Phillip asked Timothy a question. What was the question? What was Timothy's response?

Chapter 14
1. What month of the year is it now?
2. What sound did they hear? What did Timothy say it was?
3. How did Timothy prepare for the hurricane?
4. How was this storm unusual?

Study Guide Questions *The Cay*

Chapter 15
1. When did the hurricane hit?
2. What happened to the hut?
3. How long did they lie flat on the ground?
4. How did Timothy position himself and Phillip against the tree?
5. What happened to Phillip, Timothy, and Stew Cat?

Chapter 16
1. What did Phillip think about his blindness as he was burying Timothy?
2. What did Phillip do during the first three days after he had buried Timothy?
3. What did Phillip do on the fifth day?
4. Why did the birds attack Phillip?
5. How was Phillip saved from the birds?

Chapter 17
1. Phillip did something that Timothy had told him not to do. What was it?
2. Were Phillip's efforts successful?
3. What happened when Phillip put his hand into the deep hole?
4. Did Phillip ever go into the hole again?

Chapter 18
1. What did Phillip say was making up for his loss of sight?
2. What did Phillip do when he heard the airplane in early August?
3. Did the plane come to Phillip's aid?
4. What did Phillip conclude about the smoke from the signal fire, and what did he do about it?
5. Describe the events that happened on August 20, 1942.

Chapter 19
1. What sound did Phillip hear?
2. Where was the sound coming from?
3. What did Phillip take with him when he left the cay?
4. How had Phillip been rescued?
5. Did Phillip regain his sight?
6. Where did Phillip spend a lot of his time when he went back to Willemstad?
7. What does Phillip say he would like to do someday?

ANSWER KEY: SHORT ANSWER STUDY GUIDE QUESTIONS - *The Cay*

Chapter 1

1. What did Phillip do that he wasn't supposed to do?
   > He went into Punda and Ft. Amsterdam to see the U boats with Henrik.

2. Identify Henrik van Boven.
   > Henrik was Phillip's Dutch friend who was also 11 years old.

3. How was the fort different on this visit than before?
   > There were real soldiers with rifles and machine guns–not like a storybook at all. Everyone was tense. Men chased the boys away.

4. What was different at the Queen Emma pontoon bridge?
   > Ferryboats and schooners were tied up and empty. Black men were not laughing or shouting as they usually did.

5. Where did Phillip's father work?
   > He worked at the oil refinery, a prime target for enemy bombing.

6. Where were the Enrights from? What were they doing in Curacao?
   > The Enrights were from Virginia. Royal Dutch Shell had borrowed Mr. Enright for the war effort because he was an expert in gasoline production and refineries.

Chapter 2

1. What kept Phillip awake most of the night?
   > He overheard his parents' conversation and got thinking about how he would miss the island if he had to leave it.

2. Why did the Chinese crews on the tankers refuse to sail?
   > They were afraid of being torpedoed and having their ships full of fuel explode.

3. Identify SS *Empire Tern*.
   > It was one of the few armed tankers in the harbor. She was loaded with fuel. A German sub torpedoed it before it got out of the bay.

4. What effect did the sinking of the *Tern* have on Phillip?
   > "I was no longer excited about the war. I had begun to understand that it meant death and destruction."

Answer Key Short Answer Study Guide Questions *The Cay*

5. What was Phillip's reaction to his mother's telling him they were leaving the island to go home to Norfolk?
    "Suddenly I felt hollow inside. Then I became angry and accused her of being a coward. She told me to go off to school. I said I hated her."

6. Phillip didn't want to leave Curacao and thought about hiding. Why didn't he hide?
    The island was so small that there was really nowhere to hide, and he knew it would cause his father trouble.

7. Identify the SS *Hato*.
    It was a small Dutch freighter on which Phillip and his mother left for Miami.

8. Describe the parting of Phillip and his mother from his dad.
    They were sad. His dad tried to be cheerful but Phillip knew he was very worried.

Chapter 3

1. When was the *Hato* torpedoed?
    It was torpedoed at 3 A.M. on April 6, 1942, two days after leaving Panama.

2. How did Phillip and his mother get separated?
    The *Hato* lurched as they were getting into the lifeboat. The life boat tilted and the passengers ended up in the water.

3. What happened to Phillip as he went into the water?
    Phillip got hit in the head and knocked unconscious as he went into the water.

4. Describe the man Phillip saw when he came to after being hit in the head going into the water.
    "I saw a huge, very old Negro sitting on the raft near me. He was ugly. His nose was flat and his face was broad; his head was a mass of wiry gray hair."

5. Who was on the raft with Phillip?
    An old Negro man and a big black and gray cat were on the raft with him.

6. What did the Negro man call Phillip?
    He called Phillip "young bahss."

7. What happened to Phillip's mother?
    The Negro man thought she had gotten onto a raft or in a lifeboat.

Answer Key Short Answer Study Guide Questions *The Cay*

8. Identify Stew.
   Stew was the cook's cat that climbed onto the raft.

9. What "rare good luck" did Phillip and Timothy have?
   They had the raft and a keg with biscuits, chocolate, and dry matches.

10. Identify Timothy.
    Timothy was the name of the Negro man who saved Phillip on the raft.

Chapter 4
1. Where was Timothy's home?
   Timothy was from Charlotte Amalie on St. Thomas in the Virgin Islands.

2. Timothy told Phillip they had something very important to do the next day. What was it?
   Timothy said they had to stay alive.

3. The pain went away from Phillip's head, but what happened that was worse?
   He went blind.

4. What did Timothy say about Phillip's condition?
   He said that was "all natural temporary."

5. How did Phillip feel he realized his condition? What did he do?
   He felt frightened and then angry. He hit Timothy.

Chapter 5
1. What hopeful thing happened toward noon on the third day that Phillip and Timothy were on the raft?
   A plane flew over.

2. What did Timothy say was bad luck?
   The cat was bad luck, but to cause the death of a cat would be *very* bad luck.

3. What did Phillip ask Timothy to tell him? What did Timothy do?
   Phillip asked Timothy to tell him what he saw. Timothy described the sky, the water, the fish, and the birds.

4. What did Phillip wonder?
   He wondered if he would ever see a bird again.

Answer Key Short Answer Study Guide Questions *The Cay*

Chapter 6

1. What caused Phillip to fall off the raft and fall in the water with the sharks?
   Timothy shouted that he spotted land. Phillip jumped up, and in his excitement he lost his balance and fell overboard.

2. What did Timothy see that the raft was headed toward?
   He saw a small island.

3. How did Timothy and Phillip feel about leaving the raft?
   Timothy thought it was a good idea. He thought they would get help from land. Phillip wanted to stay on the raft because he thought the Navy was still searching for them.

4. What words did Phillip use to describe Timothy?
   Phillip said he didn't "think there was anyone on earth as *stubborn* as old Timothy."

Chapter 7

1. How did Phillip feel when Timothy left him alone on the beach to explore the island?
   He was frightened because he knew he was helpless without Timothy.

2. How did Timothy describe the island?
   He said it was about a mile long and a half-mile wide. It was shaped like a melon. There were sea grapes, lizards, and palm trees on the island.

3. Where did Timothy plan to make their camp?
   He wanted to make their camp on a rise near the palm trees, about 40 feet from the sea.

4. What was Timothy worried about?
   He thought they might be on one of a group of small cays. These cays were in an area called the Devil's Mouth. The cays were surrounded by coral, which made it hard to get to them.

5. How did they celebrate making landfall?
   They each had a half of a cup of water.

Chapter 8

1. How did Phillip describe the times he spent alone during the first few days on the island?
   He said they were terrible.

2. How old did Timothy say he was?
   He said he was more than seventy years old.

Answer Key Short Answer Study Guide Questions *The Cay*

3. What two things did Timothy do to alert ships and planes of their location?
    He built a fire and he spelled the word "help" on the beach with stones.

4. What did Phillip discover about Timothy as they worked?
    Timothy could not spell.

Chapter 9
1. What did Timothy make with vines, and what was it for?
    He wove a rope of vines to go from the hut to the beach and fire pile. He said it was for Phillip, so he could help with the work. He could also take a torch from the hut campfire to the fire on the beach if he heard a plane.

2. What did Timothy ask Phillip to do? ?
    Timothy asked Phillip to weave their sleeping mats.

3. Describe the scene where Phillip lost his temper about weaving the mats.
    Phillip was not able to weave the mats. He threw the palm fibers at Timothy and called him an ugly black man. Timothy slapped Phillip across the cheek.

4. Describe what happened after Phillip lost his temper.
    He realized that Timothy was making the rope for him. Phillip told Timothy he wanted to be friends. Timothy said Phillip had always been his friend.

5. What did Phillip ask Timothy to call him?
    Phillip asked Timothy to call him Phillip instead of young boss.

Chapter 10
1. What happened on their seventh night on the island, and how did they feel about it?
    It rained for two hours. They were both happy.

2. Phillip asked Timothy why there were different colors of skin. What was Timothy's answer?
    Timothy said he didn't know, but he believed that all were the same under the skin.

3. What was the problem with getting the coconuts?
    They were 40 feet of the ground. Timothy said he was too old to climb the tree, and Phillip was too afraid to climb.

4. Phillip asked Timothy how his eyes looked. What was Timothy's answer?
    Timothy said Phillip's eyes stared.

Answer Key Short Answer Study Guide Questions *The Cay*

5. Did Phillip's appearance bother Timothy?
    No. Timothy was glad to have Phillip's company.

Chapter 11
1. What did Timothy make to help Phillip get around?
    He made a cane.

2. Timothy was trying to make Phillip more independent. Phillip did not like to think about the reason. What did he say the reason was?
    Phillip knew there was a possibility that Timothy could die and leave him alone on the cay.

3. Timothy thought something was wrong with the island. What was it?
    Timothy thought the island had a jumbi, or evil spirit.

4. Why was Phillip concerned about Stew Cat?
    Timothy thought Stew Cat was bad luck. Phillip was worried that Timothy might harm or kill the cat.

5. What did Timothy do to try and change their luck?
    He put Stew Cat on the raft, away from the island. Then he carved a wooden cat and put it on top of the hut. This was supposed to scare away the jumbi.

Chapter 12
1. What happened to Timothy one morning in May?
    He got a case of malaria.

2. What did Phillip do when Timothy ran into the water?
    Phillip followed Timothy into the water and pulled him out.

3. Why did Phillip put sea grape leaves over Timothy's body?
    The leaves protected him from the sun.

4 How was Timothy when he woke up?
    The fever was gone but he never fully regained his strength.

5. How much time went by during the time of Timothy's ordeal?
    One day.

Answer Key Short Answer Study Guide Questions *The Cay*

Chapter 13

1. What did Timothy decide in late May?
    He thought they would stay on the island forever.

2. How did they keep track of the days?
    Every day Timothy put a pebble into an old can he found on the beach.

3. What did Timothy teach Phillip to do? Why did Timothy think Phillip should learn this?
    Timothy taught Phillip to fish. Timothy was afraid he might get sick again or die. He knew that Phillip must be able to feed himself.

4. How did Phillip feel about the results of Timothy's lessons?
    Phillip was happy that he learned to fish. He said, "I felt I had learned to do something very special. I was learning to do things all over again, by touch and feel."

5. What things had Timothy never thought about? What did Phillip tell him?
    Timothy had never thought about how the cay formed or how the sea grape, vines, coconuts, or lizards got there. Phillip explained the geography and probable origin of all of these things.

6. What feat did Phillip accomplish next?
    He climbed the coconut tree and pulled off two coconuts.

7. What did Timothy tell Phillip after this success?
    Timothy told Phillip he did not need his eyes. He was able to do without his eyes what Timothy could not do with his body.

8. That night, Phillip asked Timothy a question. What was the question? What was Timothy's response?
    Phillip asked Timothy if he was still black? Timothy laughed.

Chapter 14

1. What month of the year is it now?
    July

2. What sound did they hear? What did Timothy say it was?
    They heard a sound like a rifle shot. Timothy said it was the waves, warning that a hurricane was coming.

Answer Key Short Answer Study Guide Questions *The Cay*

3. How did Timothy prepare for the hurricane?
>He lashed the water keg to a palm tree trunk. He tied the rest of the rope around the tree trunk so they could hang onto it if necessary. They ate a large meal. He put his knife in the tin box and lashed the box to the tree.

4. How was this storm unusual?
>Most hurricanes occurred in September or October. Since this was a July hurricane, it was very dangerous.

Chapter 15

1. When did the hurricane hit?
>It hit after dark.

2. What happened to the hut?
>It was blown away.

3. How long did they lie flat on the ground?
>They were flat on the ground for about two hours.

4. How did Timothy position himself and Phillip against the tree?
>Phillip was against the bark of the tree. Timothy was behind him, shielding Phillip from the storm.

5. What happened to Phillip, Timothy, and Stew Cat?
>Phillip and Stew Cat survived. Timothy died.

Chapter 16

1. What did Phillip think about his blindness as he was burying Timothy?
>He thought his blindness was "protecting him from fear."

2. What did Phillip do during the first three days after he had buried Timothy?
>He found the wood, the water keg, and the tin box. He piled up wood for a new signal fire. Next he cleaned up the camp area. Then he made a bed of palm fronds. After that he found the fishing poles Timothy had made. He sharpened Timothy's knife, then stuck it in a tree so he would be able to find it.

Answer Key Short Answer Study Guide Questions *The Cay*

3. What did Phillip do on the fifth day?
> He found another can and began putting in pebbles to keep track of the days. He also found other things on the beach that he could use.

4. Why did the birds attack Phillip?
> He had unknowingly walked into their new nest.

5. How was Phillip saved from the birds?
> Stew Cat attacked the bird that was diving at Phillip and killed it.

Chapter 17

1. Phillip did something that Timothy had told him not to do. What was it?
> He dove to the bottom of the fishing hole to get some langosta.

2. Were Phillip's efforts successful?
> Yes, he caught one langosta.

3. What happened when Phillip put his hand into the deep hole?
> Something grabbed it and bit him.

4. Did Phillip ever go into the hole again?
> No, he did not.

Chapter 18

1. What did Phillip say was making up for his loss of sight?
> His senses of touch and hearing were making up for the loss of sight.

2. What did Phillip do when he heard the airplane in early August?
> He built up the signal fire. At some time earlier, he had also made a new "Help" message out of rocks on the beach.

3. Did the plane come to Phillip's aid?
> No, the plane went away.

4. What did Phillip conclude about the smoke from the signal fire, and what did he do about it?
> He thought the smoke might be white, and was getting lost in the sky. He tried using the oily sea grape leaves to make a dark smoke. That worked.

Answer Key Short Answer Study Guide Questions *The Cay*

5. Describe the events that happened on August 20, 1942.
>Phillip heard a heavy sound that he realized were explosions. He built up the signal fire with more sea grape leaves. The plane got close, but then it left. Then Phillip felt ill and lay down on his mat.

Chapter 19
1. What sound did Phillip hear?
>He heard a bell.

2. Where was the sound coming from?
>It came from a small boat that had come into the Devil's Mouth.

3. What did Phillip take with him when he left the cay?
>He took Stew Cat and Timothy's knife.

4. How had Phillip been rescued?
>The plane had seen his smoke and radioed the information to the destroyer.

5. Did Phillip regain his sight?
>Yes, after three operations in New York City he got his sight back, but he had to wear glasses.

6. Where did Phillip spend a lot of his time when he went back to Willemstad?
>He spent time along St. Anna Bay and the Ruyterkade market talking to the black people. Some of them had known Timothy.

7. What does Phillip say he would like to do someday?
>He would like to charter a boat from Panama and find the cay. Then he would stand by Timothy's grave and say, "Dis b'dat outrageous cay, eh, Timothy?"

MULTIPLE CHOICE FORMAT STUDY GUIDE/QUIZ QUESTIONS - *The Cay*

<u>Chapter 1</u>

1. What did Phillip do that he was not supposed to do?
    A. He skipped school.
    B. He went into Punda and Ft. Amsterdam with Henrik to see the U boats.
    C. He played with some of the native children.
    D. He listened to news of the war on the radio.

2. True or False: Henrik van Boven was Phillip's Dutch friend who was also 11 years old.
    A. True
    B. False

3. Which of the following is **not** one of the ways that the fort was different now?
    A. There were real soldiers with rifles and machine guns.
    B. Everyone was tense.
    C. The boys had to show identification badges to get on the fort grounds.
    D. Men chased the boys away.

4. What was different at the Queen Emma pontoon bridge?
    A. The bridge was stuck open. No one was trying to fix it.
    B. Soldiers were standing at the entrance to the bridge.
    C. The bridge had been blown up.
    D. Ferryboats and schooners were tied up and empty. Black men were not laughing and shouting.

5. Where did Phillip's father work?
    A. He worked at the oil refinery.
    B. He worked in the state department offices.
    C. He worked on one of the ferryboats.
    D. He worked for the main bank on Curaçao.

6. Where were the Enrights from?
    A. They were from England.
    B. They were from Holland.
    C. They were from Panama.
    D. They were from Virginia.

Multiple Choice Study Guide/Quiz Questions *The Cay*

7. What were they doing in Curaçao?
	A. Mrs. Enright was teaching school there.
	B. They were on vacation.
	C. Royal Dutch Shell had borrowed Mr. Enright from his regular company for the war effort.
	D. Phillip was an exchange student. His parents had gone there to get him at the end of the term.

Multiple Choice Study Guide/Quiz Questions *The Cay*

Chapter 2

1. Phillip overheard his parents' conversation about his mother wanting to leave the island. What did Phillip do in response to what he overheard?
    A. He interrupted his parents and said he would not leave.
    B. He stayed awake most of the night.
    C. He wrote a letter to his parents and put it under their bedroom door.
    D. He ran to his friend Henrik's house and cried.

2. Why did the Chinese crews on the tankers refuse to sail?
    A. They were afraid of being torpedoed and having the ships explode.
    B. They were on the side of the Germans.
    C. They had not been paid in a month and had gone on strike.
    D. The ships were old and needed to be repaired, but there was no one at the port who could do this.

3. What happened to the *SS Empire Tern*?
    A. It sank a German U-boat.
    B. It was bombed by a fighter plane.
    C. It was torpedoed by a German submarine.
    D. It got out of the harbor safely and sailed to England.

4. What effect did the episode with the *SS Empire Tern* have on Phillip?
    A. He felt pride in the sailors and the ship.
    B. He began to understand that war meant death and destruction.
    C. He feared for his father's life.
    D. He wanted to fight the Germans himself.

5. Phillip's mother told him they were leaving the island to go home to Norfolk. What did he say to her?
    A. He said they should stay for six more months before making a decision.
    B. He said he understood and would cooperate with her.
    C. He said she should go alone and he would take care of his father.
    D. He said she was a coward and he hated her.

6. True or False: Phillip did not hide because he knew it would cause trouble for his father.
    A. True
    B. False

Multiple Choice Study Guide/Quiz Questions *The Cay*

7. What was the name of the ship on which Phillip and his mother left?
    A. *SS Hato*
    B. *USS Miami*
    C. *HMS Scharloo*
    D. *RDN Van Kingsbergen*

8. How did Phillip describe his father as he was standing on the wall of Fort Amsterdam, waving to them on the ship?
    A. a brave and happy man
    B. a tall and lonely figure
    C. an angry and impatient person
    D. an encouraging and strong father

Multiple Choice Study Guide/Quiz Questions *The Cay*

<u>Chapter 3</u>

1. When was the Hato torpedoed?
    A. 2 P. M. on June 24, 1943
    B. 9 A. M. on May 19, 1944
    C. 12 P. M. on March 30, 1941
    D. 3 A. M. on April 6, 1942

2. How did Phillip and his mother get separated?
    A. The *Hato* lurched as they were getting into the lifeboat. The lifeboat tilted and the passengers landed in the water.
    B. Phillip ran back to the cabin to get something and was put in a different lifeboat.
    C. There was not enough room in the lifeboat for everyone so his mother put Phillip in and she stayed on the ship.
    D. Phillip's mother fainted on the deck of the Hato. The doctor kept her onboard to treat her. Then he put her in the lifeboat with him and the crew.

3. What happened to Phillip?
    A. He broke his right leg as he jumped from the *Hato*.
    B. He got hit on the head and knocked unconscious as he fell into the water.
    C. He sprained his shoulder from hanging onto the side of the lifeboat.
    D. His lifejacket got caught on a board, and broke three of his ribs.

4. Which of the following phrases does <u>not</u> describe the man Phillip saw?
    A. ugly
    B. flat nose and broad face
    C. short and fat
    D. wiry gray hair

5. Who was on the raft with Phillip?
    A. the Negro man and a big black and gray cat
    B. one Dutch sailor
    C. a dog and the ship's captain
    D. two other children who were also passengers on the ship

6. What did the Negro man call Phillip?
    A. Sir Phillip
    B. Your Lordship
    C. young bahss
    D. Mr. Enright's son

Multiple Choice Study Guide/Quiz Questions *The Cay*

7. What happened to Phillip's mother?
    A. She drowned.
    B. She got on a raft or in a lifeboat.
    C. The Germans captured her.
    D. She was rescued by another ship.

8. What was the name of the cat?
    A. Cookie
    B. Rascal
    C. Anna
    D. Stew

9. What items were on the raft that the man on the raft said was "rare good luck"?
    A. There was a keg of water, biscuits, chocolate, and dry matches.
    B. There were signal flares, two blankets, and several tea bags.
    C. There was a knife, a can opener, and three cans of tuna.
    D. There were two paddles, a lifejacket, and four oranges.

10. Who was Timothy?
    A. The captain of the ship
    B. The Negro man on the raft
    C. The ship's cook
    D. Phillip's father

Multiple Choice Study Guide/Quiz Questions *The Cay*

Chapter 4

1. Where was Timothy's original home?
    A. Norfolk, Virginia
    B. Charlotte Amalie on St. Thomas in the Virgin Islands
    C. London, England
    D. Aruba in the Dutch West Indies

2. Timothy told Phillip they had something very important to do. What was it?
    A. stay alive
    B. get some sleep
    C. build a shelter
    D. find land

3. The pain went away from Phillip's head. What happened next that was worse?
    A. He got a terrible sunburn.
    B. He got violently seasick.
    C. He went blind.
    D. He lost the use of his legs.

4. What did Timothy say about Phillip's condition?
    A. It was punishment because he was angry with his mother.
    B. It was not as bad as it could have been.
    C. It was terrible misfortune.
    D. It was natural and temporary.

5. How did Phillip feel when he realized his condition?
    A. frightened and then angry
    B. glad it was not worse
    C. optimistic that he would get better
    D. confused

6. What did Phillip do when he realized his condition?
    A. He jumped into the water.
    B. He screamed and cried.
    C. He hit Timothy.
    D. He banged his head on the raft.

Multiple Choice Study Guide/Quiz Questions *The Cay*

Chapter 5

1. What hopeful thing happened on the third day they were on the raft?
    A. A large fish jumped onto the raft, and they ate it.
    B. A plane flew over.
    C. They saw a ship on the horizon.
    D. It was cloudy so they were protected from the hot sun.

2. What did Timothy say was bad luck?
    A. Phillip was thirteen, and thirteen was an unlucky number.
    B. The wind was blowing them out to sea instead of towards land.
    C. The cat was bad luck, but to cause its death would be *very* bad luck.
    D. They had not seen any dolphins. Dolphins were good luck.

3. What did Phillip ask Timothy to tell him?
    A. Phillip asked Timothy to tell him what he saw.
    B. Phillip asked Timothy to tell him a story from his childhood.
    C. Phillip asked Timothy to tell him what had happened when the boat sank.
    D. Phillip asked Timothy to tell him how he thought they might get rescued.

4. What did Phillip wonder?
    A. He wondered if they would survive.
    B. He wondered if the headache would return.
    C. He wondered how long they had been on the raft.
    D. He wondered if he would ever see a bird again.

Multiple Choice Study Guide/Quiz Questions *The Cay*

<u>Chapter 6</u>

1. Timothy shouted that he had seen land. What did Phillip do?
    A. He started singing.
    B. He jumped up and fell off the raft.
    C. He began paddling with both arms.
    D. He hugged Timothy.

2. What was in the water around the raft?
    A. sharks
    B. dolphins
    C. seaweed
    D. debris from the ship

3. Which statement is true?
    A. Both Phillip and Timothy wanted to get to land.
    B. Phillip wanted to get to land but Timothy wanted to stay on the raft.
    C. Phillip wanted to stay on the raft but Timothy wanted to get onto land.
    D. Both Phillip and Timothy wanted to stay on the raft.

4. What word did Phillip use to describe Timothy?
    A. wise
    B. energetic
    C. brave
    D. stubborn

Multiple Choice Study Guide/Quiz Questions *The Cay*

Chapter 7

1. What made Phillip feel frightened?
  A. He did not know what they would eat.
  B. Timothy left him alone on the beach.
  C. He could not swim.
  D. He was afraid of lizards.

2. What did the island look like?
  A. It was five miles long, two miles wide, pear-shaped and had no trees.
  B. It was a circle with a diameter of three miles, with trees on one side.
  C. It was one mile long, a half-mile wide, with sea grapes and palm trees.
  D. It was two miles long and covered with rocks.

3. True or False: Timothy wanted to make their camp on a rise about 40 feet from the sea.
  A. True
  B. False

4. What was Timothy worried about?
  A. He thought the island might be an ancient burial ground, which was bad luck.
  B. He thought the island was unstable and might sink.
  C. He thought there might be pirates on the island.
  D. He thought the island might be hard to get to because of surrounding coral.

5. What was the name Timothy called the area where the island was?
  A. Calypso Cays
  B. Devil's Mouth
  C. Sailor's Paradise
  D. Leeward Isles

6. How did they celebrate making land?
  A. They each had a half of a cup of water.
  B. They ate a chocolate bar.
  C. They danced on the beach.
  D. They said a prayer.

Multiple Choice Study Guide/Quiz Questions *The Cay*

Chapter 8

1. How did Phillip describe the times he spent alone during the first few days on the island?
    A. He said they were exciting.
    B. He said they were interesting.
    C. He said they were terrible.
    D. He said they were boring.

2. How old did Timothy say he was?
    A. about fifty
    B. more than seventy
    C. just about forty
    D. a little less than sixty

3. What two things did Timothy do to alert ships to their location?
    A. He built a signal fire and spelled the word "help" on the beach with stones.
    B. He hung a white cloth from one of the palm trees and built a signal fire.
    C. He built a tower of stones and shells and pulled the raft onto the sand.
    D. He spelled the words "save us" on the beach with shells and set fire to the palm trees.

4. What did Phillip discover about Timothy as they worked?
    A. Timothy could speak four languages.
    B. Timothy had been a prizefighter when he was younger.
    C. Timothy could not spell.
    D. Timothy had a grandson who was the same age as Phillip.

Multiple Choice Study Guide/Quiz Questions *The Cay*

<u>Chapter 9</u>

1. What did Timothy make next for Phillip?
    A. He made a pair of sunglasses from seashells.
    B. He made a cape from palm fronds.
    C. He made sandals from pieces of driftwood.
    D. He made a rope of vines from the hut to the beach and fire pile.

2. What did Timothy ask Phillip to do?
    A. He asked Phillip to weave their sleeping mats.
    B. He asked Phillip to cook dinner.
    C. He asked Phillip to gather shells.
    D. He asked Phillip to wash their clothes.

3. True or False: Phillip politely did what Timothy asked him to do.
    A. True
    B. False

4. How did Timothy respond to Phillip's actions?
    A. He told Phillip to stay in the hut alone for a while.
    B. He threatened to leave the island.
    C. He slapped Phillip across the cheek.
    D. He ignored Phillip.

5. True or False: Phillip told Timothy he wanted to be friends.
    A. True
    B. False

6. What did Phillip ask Timothy to call him?
    A. young boss
    B. Master Enright
    C. grandson
    D. Phillip

Multiple Choice Study Guide/Quiz Questions *The Cay*

Chapter 10

1. What happened on their seventh night on the island, and how did they feel about it?
    A. It rained for two hours and they were happy.
    B. Timothy recognized several constellations and was happy that he knew where they were.
    C. They heard loud screeching noises and were very scared.
    D. Stew stole their dinner and they were both angry with him.

2. Phillip asked Timothy why there were different colors of skin. What was Timothy's answer?
    A. He said it was because the sun in some areas made people darker.
    B. He said he didn't know, but he believed all were the same under the skin.
    C. He said it was a curse put upon people by a devil.
    D. He said it was a challenge to make people work together.

3. Why couldn't they get the coconuts?
    A. There were monkeys in the trees guarding the coconuts.
    B. They were not ripe yet.
    C. Timothy was too old to climb the tree and Phillip was afraid.
    D. The tree was not strong enough to hold the weight of a person.

4. Phillip asked Timothy how his eyes looked. What was Timothy's answer?
    A. He said Phillip's eyes were bloodshot.
    B. He said Phillip's eyes were shut tight.
    C. He said Phillip's eyes rolled around in his head.
    D. He said Phillip's eyes stared.

5. True or False: Phillip's appearance bothered Timothy.
    A. True
    B. False

Multiple Choice Study Guide/Quiz Questions *The Cay*

Chapter 11
1. What did Timothy make for Phillip?
    A. a hat
    B. a cane
    C. a spear
    D. a fork

2. Phillip knew that Timothy was trying to make him more independent in case ___
    A. Timothy became too weak to work.
    B. Timothy lost his sight, too.
    C. Timothy died.
    D. Timothy got tired of doing all the work.

3. Timothy thought the island had a jumbi. What is that?
    A. an evil spirit
    B. an active volcano
    C. a gold mine
    D. a pond of poisonous water

4. Why was Phillip concerned about Stew Cat?
    A. There was nothing on the island for the cat to eat and he was starving.
    B. The cat was getting very wild and unfriendly.
    C. Phillip thought the cat was sick and he had no way to treat the illness.
    D. Timothy thought the cat was bad luck. Phillip thought Timothy might hurt the cat.

5. What did Timothy do to try and change their luck?
    A. He made Stew Cat stay away from their hut.
    B. He carved a wooden cat and put it on top of the hut.
    C. He said magic words to keep away the bad luck.
    D. He built a high wall of sand on the beach.

Multiple Choice Study Guide/Quiz Questions *The Cay*

Chapter 12

1. What happened to Timothy one morning in May?
    A. He cut his leg with his knife.
    B. He stepped on a piece of coral and hurt his foot.
    C. He got malaria.
    D. He had a toothache and had to pull out his tooth.

2. True or False: When Timothy ran into the water, Phillip let him stay there.
    A. True
    B. False

3. What did Phillip use to protect Timothy's body?
    A. sea grape leaves
    B. sand
    C. palm fronds
    D. shells and stones

4. Did Timothy ever fully regain his strength?
    A. Yes
    B. No

5. How much time when by during the time of Timothy's ordeal?
    A. four days
    B. seven days
    C. three days
    D. one day

Multiple Choice Study Guide/Quiz Questions *The Cay*

Chapter 13

1. What did Timothy decide in late May?
	A. They would stay on the island forever.
	B. They should go back onto the raft and look for help.
	C. Rescuers would be coming any day now.
	D. They would be dead within a month.

2. How did they keep track of the days?
	A. Timothy put notches in a stick.
	B. They said the day and date aloud every morning.
	C. They made a mark on the raft with a seashell.
	D. Timothy put a pebble in an old can every day.

3. What did Timothy teach Phillip to do?
	A. He taught Phillip to speak Dutch.
	B. He taught Phillip to fish.
	C. He taught Phillip to swim.
	D. He taught Phillip to make tools with stones.

4. Phillip said, ". . . I was learning to do things all over again, by ____"
	A. myself.
	B. using my head.
	C. touch and feel.
	D. trusting someone else.

5. What did Phillip explain to Timothy?
	A. the geography and probable origin of the things on the island
	B. the water cycle
	C. the use of the North Star to navigate on the sea
	D. the sounds and names of the letters of the alphabet

6. What feat did Phillip accomplish next?
	A. He swam around the island.
	B. He cooked dinner by himself.
	C. He caught lizards with his bare hands.
	D. He climbed the palm tree and got two coconuts.

Multiple Choice Study Guide/Quiz Questions *The Cay*

7. After this success, Timothy said Phillip did not need ___
    A. him (Timothy) to help him anymore.
    B. his eyes.
    C. to be rescued.
    D. any more lessons.

8. That night, Phillip asked Timothy a question. What was it?
    A. "Are you still black?
    B. "When will we be rescued?"
    C. "What will I do if you die?"
    D. "Will you live with me when we get home?"

Multiple Choice Study Guide/Quiz Questions *The Cay*

Chapter 14

1. What month of the year is it now?
 A. September
 B. December
 C. July
 D. April

2. What sound did they hear?
 A. a shot
 B. a screech
 C. a crash
 D. a buzz

3. What did Timothy say the sound was?
 A. thunder
 B. the waves
 C. the palm trees
 D. rocks crashing against each other

4. What did Timothy say was coming?
 A. a volcanic eruption
 B. an earthquake
 C. a blizzard
 D. a hurricane

5. True or False: In preparation for the upcoming event, Timothy put all of their supplies on the raft.
 A. True
 B. False

6. True or False: Timothy said this was a very unusual event for the time of year.
 A. True
 B. False

Multiple Choice Study Guide/Quiz Questions *The Cay*

Chapter 15
1. When did the hurricane hit?
   A. at dawn
   B. at noon
   C. after dark
   D. in mid-morning

2. What blew away?
   A. the hut
   B. one of the palm trees
   C. the raft
   D. the water keg

3. How long did they lie flat on the ground?
   A. nine hours
   B. two hours
   C. four hours
   D. one hour

4. How were Timothy and Phillip positioned at the palm tree?
   A. They were standing on opposite sides of the tree.
   B. Phillip was high up on the trunk and Timothy was at the base.
   C. They were both up at the top.
   D. Phillip was against the bark and Timothy was up against his back.

5. What happened at the end of the storm?
   A. Phillip and Stew Cat survived, but Timothy died.
   B. Phillip and Timothy survived, but Stew Cat died.
   C. They were all fine.
   D. Timothy and Stew Cat were fine, but Phillip was injured.

Multiple Choice Study Guide/Quiz Questions *The Cay*

Chapter 16

1. True or False: As he was burying Timothy, Phillip thought his blindness was making his fear even worse.
    A. True
    B. False

2. What did Phillip do during the first three days after Timothy died?
    A. He sat and cried.
    B. He fixed up the camp and built a new signal fire.
    C. He slept almost all the time.
    D. He carved a new wooden cat to chase off the evil spirits.

3. What did Phillip do on the fifth day?
    A. He fixed the raft.
    B. He climbed the palm tree and got more coconuts.
    C. He found a can and started putting in pebbles to keep track of time.
    D. He used stones and seashells to build a marker for Timothy's grave.

4. What attacked Phillip?
    A. birds
    B. mosquitoes
    C. lizards
    D. fire ants

5. True or False: The creatures attacked because Phillip had accidentally disturbed their nest.
    A. True
    B. False

6. How was Phillip saved from the creatures?
    A. He lit a torch and scared them away with the fire.
    B. He ran into the water and stayed there until the disappeared.
    C. He screamed and scared them away.
    D. Stew Cat attacked the creature that was attacking Phillip.

Multiple Choice Study Guide/Quiz Questions *The Cay*

Chapter 17

1. Philip did something that Timothy told him never to do. What was it?
    A. He stayed up all night
    B. He dove to the bottom of the fishing hole.
    C. He walked on top of the coral.
    D. He moved his camp to the beach.

2. Were Phillip's efforts successful?
    A. Yes
    B. No

3. What happened to Phillip?
    A. He fell and cut his legs.
    B. He almost drowned.
    C. Something bit him on the arm.
    D. Nothing bad happened. He was fine.

4. Did Phillip ever repeat the action that Timothy told him not to do?
    A. Yes
    B. No

Multiple Choice Study Guide/Quiz Questions *The Cay*

<u>Chapter 18</u>
1. What did Phillip say about his loss of sight?
    A. His senses of touch and hearing were making up for it.
    B. He did not think he could survive much longer without it.
    C. He thought he would be even lonelier if he could see how deserted he was.
    D. He did not understand why he was being punished this way.

2. What did Phillip do when he heard the airplane in early August?
    A. He climbed to the top of the palm tree and waved.
    B. He built up the signal fire.
    C. He jumped up and down on the beach.
    D. He threw shells into the air.

3. Had Phillip made another "help" sign on the beach with stones?
    A. Yes
    B. No

4. Did the plane come to Phillip's aid?
    A. Yes
    B. No

5. What did Phillip conclude about the signal fire?
    A. The smoke was white and was getting lost in the sky.
    B. The fire was in the wrong place to be seen.
    C. It would die out soon because there weren't many palm leaves left to burn.
    D. It needed to be twice as big.

6. What did Phillip do about the fire?
    A. He put it out for good.
    B. He moved it to the other side of the island.
    C. He used oily sea grape leaves for fuel.
    D. He built a second fire about a half-mile away.

7. Phillip signaled when he heard a second plane. Did that plane come to get him?
    A. Yes
    B. No

Multiple Choice Study Guide/Quiz Questions *The Cay*

8. What was the date when Phillip heard the second plane?
- A. September 5, 1943
- B. July 4, 1944
- C. October 22, 1941
- D. August 20, 1942

Multiple Choice Study Guide/Quiz Questions *The Cay*

<u>Chapter 19</u>

1. What sound did Phillip hear?
    A. a bell
    B. a thud
    C. music
    D. a horn

2. True or False: Someone parachuted onto the island from a plane.
    A. True
    B. False

3. Phillip took Stew Cat and one other thing when he left. What was it?
    A. a coconut
    B. a fishing pole
    C. Timothy's knife
    D. the can of pebbles

4. True or False: The plane's pilot had seen the smoke from the fire and signaled a ship.
    A. True
    B. False

5. Did Phillip regain his sight?
    A. Yes
    B. No

6. Where did Phillip spend a lot of his time when he went back to Willemstad?
    A. in the hospital
    B. at the office with his father
    C. along the bay and the market
    D. with his friend

7. To whom did Phillip talk when he was back in Willemstad?
    A. blind children
    B. black people
    C. the police
    D. the sailors

8. True or False: Phillip said he never wanted to see the cay again.
    A. True
    B. False

ANSWER KEY - MULTIPLE CHOICE STUDY/QUIZ QUESTIONS
The Cay

Ch. 1	Ch. 2	Ch. 3	Ch. 4	Ch. 5	Ch. 6	Ch. 7
1. B	1. B	1. D	1. B	1. B	1. B	1. B
2. A	2. A	2. A	2. A	2. C	2. A	2. C
3. A	3. C	3. B	3. C	3. A	3. C	3. A
4. D	4. B	4. C	4. D	4. D	4. D	4. D
5. A	5. D	5. A	5. A			5. B
6. D	6. A	6. C	6. C			6. A
7. C	7. A	7. B				
	8. B	8. D				
		9. A				
		10. B				

Ch. 8	Ch. 9	Ch. 10	Ch. 11	Ch. 12	Ch. 13	Ch. 14
1. C	1. D	1. A	1. B	1. C	1. A	1. C
2. B	2. A	2. B	2. C	2. B	2. D	2. A
3. A	3. B	3. C	3. A	3. A	3. B	3. B
4. C	4. C	4. D	4. D	4. B	4. C	4. D
	5. A	5. B	5. B	5. D	5. A	5. B
	6. D				6. D	6. A
					7. B	
					8. A	

Ch. 15	Ch. 16	Ch. 17	Ch. 18	Ch. 19
1. C	1. B	1. B	1. A	1. A
2. A	2. B	2. A	2. B	2. B
3. B	3. C	3. C	3. A	3. C
4. C	4. A	4. B	4. B	4. A
5. A	5. A		5. A	5. A
	6. D		6. C	6. C
			7. B	7. B
			8. D	8. B

PREREADING VOCABULARY WORKSHEETS

VOCABULARY - *The Cay* Chapters 1-2

Part I: Using Prior Knowledge and Contextual Clues

Below are the sentences in which the vocabulary words appear in the text. Read the sentence. Use any clues you can find in the sentence combined with your prior knowledge, and write what you think the italicized words mean in the space provided.

1. [the city] looks like Holland, except that all the houses are painted in soft colors, pinks and greens and blues, and there are no ***dikes***.

   _____

2. [the Queen Emma pontoon bridge] ***spans*** the channel that leads to the huge harbor.

   _____

3. Henrik had an ***irritating*** way of sounding official since his father was connected with the government.

   _____

4. Royal Dutch Shell had borrowed him because he was an expert in refineries and gasoline production.

   _____

5. I loved the koenoekoe with its giant cactus; the divi-divi trees, their odd branches all on the ***leeward*** side of the trunk.

   _____

6. They were angry with the Chinese crews [for refusing to sail], and on the third day, my father said that ***mutiny*** charges had been placed against them.

   _____

7. The big tankers from the United States or England always carried fresh water to us in ballast, and then it was ***distilled*** again so that we could drink it.

   _____

The Cay Vocabulary Chapters 1-2 Continued

Part II: Determining the Meaning
Match the vocabulary words to their dictionary definitions.

___ 1. dikes   A. purified by boiling and condensing the vapor
___ 2. span   B. place for processing raw materials such as oil or sugar
___ 3. irritating   C. away from the wind
___ 4. refinery   D. extend over or across something
___ 5. leeward   E. embankments to prevent flooding
___ 6. mutiny   F. annoying
___ 7. distilled   G. creating an organized rebellion against a legal authority

VOCABULARY *The Cay* Chapters 3-5

Part I: Using Prior Knowledge and Contextual Clues
Below are the sentences in which the vocabulary words appear in the text. Read the sentence. Use any clues you can find in the sentence combined with your prior knowledge, and write what you think the italicized words mean in the space provided.

1. We could hear the ship's whistle blowing constantly, and there were sounds of metal ***wrenching*** and much shouting. The whole ship was shuddering.

   _____

2. His face couldn't have been blacker, or his teeth whiter. They made an ***alabaster*** trench in his mouth, and his pink-purple lips peeled back over them like the meat of a conch shell.

   _____

3. Muscles rippled over the ***ebony*** of his arms and around his shoulders.

   _____

4. I asked him for a drink of water. He nodded agreeably, saying, "D'sun do ***parch***."

   _____

5. I woke up when there was a pale band of light to the east, and Timothy said, "You ***fare*** well, young bahss? How is d'ead?"

   _____

Part II: Determining the Meaning
Match the vocabulary words to their dictionary definitions.

___ 1. wrenching   A. dry out
___ 2. alabaster   B. pulling or twisting away
___ 3. ebony   C. manage in doing something
___ 4. parch   D. brownish black color
___ 5. fare   E. type of gypsum (white mineral) usually used for decorative plaster work

VOCABULARY - *The Cay* Chapters 6-9

Part I: Using Prior Knowledge and Contextual Clues
Below are the sentences in which the vocabulary words appear in the text. Read the sentence. Use any clues you can find in the sentence combined with your prior knowledge, and write what you think the italicized words mean in the space provided.

1. The warm sand did feel good on my feet, and now I was almost glad that we wouldn't have to spend another night on the hard, wet, boards of the raft. . . . Timothy said, "'Tis a beautiful *cay*, dis cay."

   _____

2. Several small islands tucked up inside great banks of coral that made ***navigation*** dangerous was what I finally decided on.

   _____

3. "If we are in the Devil's Mouth, how can we be rescued?" . . . Finally he said, "True, but we cannot *fret* 'bout it, can we? We'll make camp and see what 'appens."

   _____

4. He was busy making a hut of dried palm ***fronds***.

   _____

5. There was a silence until Timothy broke it with ***anguish***. "Wid d'rock, say 'help.'" I looked up in his direction and suddenly understood that Timothy could not spell. He was just too stubborn, or too proud, to admit it.

   _____

6. . . . he stood above me, watching. He kept ***murmuring***, "Ah-huh, ah-huh," as if making sure I was spelling it correctly.

   _____

The Cay Vocabulary Chapters 6-9 Continued

Part II: Determining the Meaning
Match the vocabulary words to their dictionary definitions.

___ 1. cay   A. worry
___ 2. navigation   B. small, low island
___ 3. fret   C. extreme anxiety
___ 4. fronds   D. saying something softly
___ 5. anguish   E. large, divided leaves
___ 6. murmuring   F. directing a vehicle's course

VOCABULARY - *The Cay* Chapters 10-12

Part I: Using Prior Knowledge and Contextual Clues
Below are the sentences in which the vocabulary words appear in the text. Read the sentence. Use any clues you can find in the sentence combined with your prior knowledge, and write what you think the italicized words mean in the space provided.

1. Timothy yelled that his **catchment** was working. He had taken more boards from the top of the raft and had made a large trough that would catch the rain.

   _____

2. I wondered how my eyes looked and asked Timothy about that. "Dey look widout **cease**," he said. "Dey stare, Phill-eep."

   _____

3. On one end, to the east, was a low coral reef that extended several hundred yards, **awash** in many places.

   _____

4. Once, I went down to east beach, to sit near the signal fire, hoping to hear the **drone** of an aircraft.

   _____

5. I knew that if I kept going that way, I'd touch or fall over the length of lifeline rope that **tethered** the raft. Timothy had driven a heavy piece of driftwood into the sand so that the raft would not go out to sea with the tide.

   _____

6. Fever! **Malaria**! I reached over to touch him. His forehead was burning hot.

   _____

The Cay Vocabulary Chapters 10-12 Continued

Part II: Determining the Meaning
Match the vocabulary words to their dictionary definitions.

___ 1. catchment   A. recurring illness transmitted by infected mosquitoes. Common in hot countries. Characterized by fever & chills.
___ 2. cease   B. tied to
___ 3. awash   C. covered in water
___ 4. drone   D. stop
___ 5. tethered   E. device for collecting rain water
___ 6. malaria   F. low, humming sound

VOCABULARY - *The Cay* Chapters 13-15

Part I: Using Prior Knowledge and Contextual Clues

Below are the sentences in which the vocabulary words appear in the text. Read the sentence. Use any clues you can find in the sentence combined with your prior knowledge, and write what you think the italicized words mean in the space provided.

1. By now, my feet were tough and I hardly felt the jagged edges of the coral. But I knew that lurking in the tide pools were the ***treacherous*** sea urchins. Stepping on them invited a sharp spine in your foot

   _____

2. Every two feet, Timothy had driven a piece of driftwood into the coral ***crevices*** so that I could feel them as I went along.

   _____

3. He ***unraveled*** a lifeline from the raft to make single strands for the fishing line.

   _____

4. After the third morning, he let me go out alone on the reef. I'd feel my way along his driftwood ***stobs***, find the hole, pry a mussel loose, and then fish.

   _____

5. I had now been with him every moment of the day and night for two months, but I had not seen him. I remembered that ugly ***welted*** face.

   _____

6. North beach was a very strange beach anyway. The sand on it felt ***coarse*** to my feet.

   _____

7. At sunset, with the air heavy and hot, Timothy described the sky to me. He said it was flaming read and that there were thing ***veils*** of high clouds.

   _____

The Cay Vocabulary Chapters 13-15 Continued

8. Timothy was taking the full blows of the storm, sheltering me with his body. When the water *receded*, it would tug at us, and Timothy's strength would fight against it.

_____

9. It was strange and *eerie* in the eye of the hurricane. I knew we were surrounded on all sides by violent winds, but the little cay was calm and quiet.

_____

Part II: Determining the Meaning
Match the vocabulary words to their dictionary definitions.

___ 1. treacherous   A. unnerving or unusual in a way that suggests a connection with the supernatural

___ 2. crevices   B. having ridges or bumps on the skin caused by being struck by something (like a whip)

___ 3. unraveled   C. stakes

___ 4. stobs   D. rough

___ 5. welted   E. went back or further away

___ 6. coarse   F. curtain-like things

___ 7. veils   G. took apart; unwound

___ 8. receded   H. involving hidden dangers or hazards

___ 9. eerie   I. narrow cracks

VOCABULARY - *The Cay* Chapters 16-19

Part I: Using Prior Knowledge and Contextual Clues
Below are the sentences in which the vocabulary words appear in the text. Read the sentence. Use any clues you can find in the sentence combined with your prior knowledge, and write what you think the italicized words mean in the space provided.

1. In the afternoon, I *groped* west along the hill.

   _____

2. I found, on opening the bung, that the water was still sweet and that the matches, wrapped in ***cellophane***, inside the tin box, were dry.

   _____

3. Feeling it everywhere under my feet, I knew that the cay was littered with ***debris***. I started cleaning the camp area, or what was left of it. I piled all the palm fronds, frayed by the wind, in one place; sticks of wet driftwood in another.

   _____

4. Then I remembered Timothy saying that he would put [the fishing poles] in a safe place. And there they were! Not two or three, but at least a dozen, lashed together, each with a barbed hook and bolt sinker. There were one more part of the ***legacy*** Timothy had left me.

   _____

5. I accomplished a lot in three days, even putting a new edge on Timothy's knife by ***honing*** it on coral.

   _____

6. On the fifth day after the storm, I began to ***scour*** the island to find out what had been cast up.

   _____

7. I kicked and rose to the surface, the thing still on my wrist, its teeth sunk in deep. I'm sure I screamed as I broke water, ***flailing*** toward the edge of the hole.

   _____

The Cay Vocabulary Chapters 16-19 Continued

8. I heard the sound going away. Soon, it had ***vanished*** completely.

_____

9. I heard the bell again; then the engine went into reverse, the propeller thrashing. . . .
   The engine was now ***idling***, and someone was coming toward me.

_____

Part II: Determining the Meaning
Match the vocabulary words to their dictionary definitions.

___ 1. groped   A. search for something carefully
___ 2. cellophane   B. sharpening
___ 3. debris   C. disappeared
___ 4. legacy   D. thin, transparent, waterproof material made from wood pulp
___ 5. scour   E. thrashing or moving around violently
___ 6. honing   F. operating, but not in gear
___ 7. flailing   G. searched by feeling
___ 8. vanished   H. fragments of broken things
___ 9. idling   I. something inherited

ANSWER KEY - VOCABULARY *The Cay*

Chapters 1-2
1. E
2. D
3. F
4. B
5. C
6. G
7. A

Chapters 3-5
1. B
2. E
3. D
4. A
5. C

Chapters 6-9
1. B
2. F
3. A
4. E
5. C
6. D

Chapters 10-12
1. E
2. D
3. C
4. F
5. B
6. A

Chapters 13-15
1. H
2. I
3. G
4. C
5. B
6. D
7. F
8. E
9. A

Chapters 16-19
1. G
2. D
3. H
4. I
5. A
6. B
7. E
8. C
9. F

DAILY LESSON PLANS

LESSON ONE

Objectives
1. To introduce the *The Cay* unit
2. To relate prior knowledge to the new material
3. To distribute books and other related materials (study guides, reading assignments)
4. To do the pre-reading work for Chapters 1-2

Activity #1

Show students a map that includes Europe and North America. Have students locate the following places: the islands of Aruba and Curaçao; Willemstad; the Netherlands; Germany; Miami, Florida; Norfolk, Virginia; Panama; and Lake Maracaibo in Venezuela. Tell students the novel takes place in the Caribbean Sea area during World War II. Show some pictures of the islands of Aruba and Curaçao from this time period. Explain that during the war, German submarines were patrolling the waters. They destroyed, or attempted to destroy, any ships they found.

Related Links: www.curacao.com   www.uboat.net

Activity #2

Do a group KWL Sheet with the students. Some students will know something about Theodore Taylor or *The Cay* and will have information to share. Put this information in the K column (What I Know). Ask students what they want to find out from reading the book and record this in the W column (What I Want to Find Out). Keep the sheet and refer back to it after reading the book. Complete the L column (What I Learned) at that time.

Activity #3

Distribute the materials students will use in this unit. Explain in detail how students are to use these materials.

Study Guides Students should preview the study guide questions before each reading assignment to get a feeling for what events and ideas are important in that section. After reading the section, students will (as a class or individually) answer the questions to review the important events and ideas from that section of the book. Students should keep the study guides as study materials for the unit test.

Reading / Writing Assignment Sheet You (the teacher) need to fill in the reading and writing assignment sheet to let students know when their reading has to be completed. You can either write the assignment sheet on a side blackboard or bulletin board and leave it there for students to see each day, or you can duplicate copies for each student to have. In either case, you should advise students to become very familiar with the reading assignments so they know what is expected of them.

Unit Outline You may find it helpful to distribute copies of the Unit Outline to your students so they can keep track of upcoming lessons and assignments. You may also want to post a copy of the Unit Outline on a bulletin board and cross off each lesson as you complete it.

Extra Activities Center The Unit Resource Materials portion of this unit contains suggestions for a library of related books and articles in your classroom as well as crossword and word search puzzles. Make an extra activities center in your room where you will keep these materials for students to use. Bring the books and articles in from the library and keep several copies of the puzzles on hand. Explain to students that these materials are available for students to use when they finish reading assignments or other class work early.

Books Each school has its own rules and regulations regarding student use of school books. Advise students of the procedures that are normal for your school.

Notebook or Unit Folder You may want the students to keep all of their worksheets, notes, and other papers for the unit together in a binder or notebook. During the first class meeting, tell them how you want them to arrange the folder. Make divider pages for vocabulary worksheets, pre-reading study guide questions, review activities, notes, and tests. You may want to give a grade for accuracy in keeping the folder.

Activity #4

Show students how to preview the study questions and do the vocabulary work for chapters 1-2 of *The Cay*. If students do not finish this assignment in class, they should complete it prior to the next class meeting.

KWL Worksheet
The Cay

Directions: Before reading, think about what you already know about Theodore Taylor and/or *The Cay*. Write the information in the **K** column. Think about what you would like to find out from reading the book. Write your questions in the **W** column. After you have read the book, use the **L** column to write the answers to your questions from the W column, and anything else you remember from the book.

K What I Know	**W** What I Want to Find Out	**L** What I Learned

LESSON TWO

Objectives
1. To read Chapters 1-2
2. To review the main ideas and events from Chapters 1-2
3. To become acquainted with the non-fiction reading assignment.

Activity #1

You may want to read Chapter 1 aloud to the students to set the mood for the novel. Invite willing students to read Chapter 2 aloud to the rest of the class. Students with some acting ability may enjoy the challenge of taking the parts of the characters and reading the dialogue. If this is done, also have a student read the narrative portions of the text.

Note: Explain that Scharloo is a neighborhood in Willemstad. During the time of World War II, it was where the wealthy people lived.

Activity #2

Give the students time to answer the study guide questions, and then discuss the answers in detail. Write the answers on the board or overhead projector film so students can have the correct answers for study purposes. Encourage students to take notes. If the students own their books, encourage them to use highlighters or colored pens to mark important passages and the answers to the study guide questions.

Note: it is a good practice in public speaking and leadership skills for individual students to take charge of leading the discussion of the study questions. Perhaps a different student could go to the front of the class and lead the discussion each day that they study questions are discussed during the unit. Of course, the teacher should guide the discussion when appropriate and be sure to fill in any gaps the students leave.

Activity #3

Distribute copies of the Non-fiction Assignment sheet and go over it in detail with the students. Explain to students that they each are to read at least one nonfiction piece at some time during the unit. This could be a book, a magazine article, or information from an encyclopedia or the Internet. Students will fill out a non-fiction assignment sheet after completing the reading to help you (the teacher) evaluate their reading experiences and to help the students think about and evaluate their own reading experiences. Give them the due date for the assignment (Lesson 15.)

Encourage students to read about topics that are related to the theme of the novel. Some suggestions are: wilderness survival, shipwreck survival; physical characteristics of the Caribbean Islands and the Dutch West Indies; hurricanes and their effects; World War II, especially the Germans' use of submarines and U-boats to destroy Allied vessels; and the petroleum industry in Aruba and Curaçao.

NON-FICTION ASSIGNMENT *The Cay*
(To be completed after reading the required nonfiction article)

Name _____ Date _____ Class _____

Title of Nonfiction Read _____

Written By _____ Publication Date _____

Web Site Address (if applicable) _____

I. Factual Summary: Write a short summary of the piece you read.

II. Vocabulary:
    1. Which vocabulary words were difficult?

    2. What did you do to help yourself understand the words?

III. Interpretation: What was the main point the author wanted you to get from reading his/her work?

IV. Criticism:
    1. Which points of the piece did you agree with or find easy to believe? Why?

    2. With which points of the piece did you disagree or find difficult to believe? Why?

V. Personal Response:
    1. What do you think about this piece?

    2. How does this piece help you better understand the novel *The Cay*?

LESSON THREE

Objectives
1. To do the pre-reading and vocabulary work for chapters 3-5
2. To understand and identify the use of dialect
3. To read chapters 3-5
4. To practice reading orally
5. To have students' oral reading evaluated

Activity #1
Give students ten or fifteen minutes to complete the pre-reading vocabulary worksheet and preview the study guide questions.

Activity #2
Explain to students that one character, Timothy, speaks in a dialect. A dialect is a way of speaking that is common to a particular area or group of people. Timothy uses a dialect that is common among the black population of the Virgin Islands. His words are written as he would have said them. For example, the word "bahss" means "boss." Encourage students to read the words as they are written to get the flavor of the dialect.

Activity #3
Tell students their oral reading ability will be evaluated. Show them copies of the Oral Reading Evaluation Form and discuss it. Model correct intonation and expression by reading the first few paragraphs of Chapter 3 aloud.

Activity #4
Call on individual students to read a few paragraphs aloud. Encourage the other students to follow along silently in their books. If you have a student who is unwilling or unable to read in front of the group make arrangements to do his or her evaluation privately at another time. Mark the oral reading evaluation forms as the students read. If all students have read orally before the chapters have been completed, assign the remainder of the text as individual silent reading.

Activity #5
Tell students they will have a quiz on chapters 1-5 during the next class period. Encourage them to complete the reading and go over the vocabulary and study question worksheets they have done.

ORAL READING EVALUATION *The Cay*

Name   Class   Date _____

SKILL	EXCELLENT	GOOD	AVERAGE	FAIR	POOR
FLUENCY	5	4	3	2	1
CLARITY	5	4	3	2	1
AUDIBILITY	5	4	3	2	1
PRONUNCIATION	5	4	3	2	1
_____	5	4	3	2	1
_____	5	4	3	2	1

TOTAL _____ **GRADE** _____

COMMENTS:

LESSON FOUR

Objectives
1. To demonstrate understanding of the main ideas and events from chapters 1-5
2. To do the pre-reading and vocabulary work for chapters 6-9
3. To begin to identify examples of character development
4. To read chapters 6-9

Activity #1
Quiz--Distribute quizzes (multiple choice study questions for chapters 1-5) and give students about fifteen minutes to complete them. Correct and grade the papers as a class. You may want to have students exchange papers, or allow them to correct their own work. As an extra credit assignment, have students find the correct answers to any questions they missed. Collect the quizzes for recording the grades.

Activity #2
Give students about fifteen minutes to preview the study questions for chapters 6-9 and do the related vocabulary work.

Activity #3 Mini-lesson: Character Traits
Explain that an author creates a character, by giving him traits such as physical attributes, thoughts, and feelings. Words to describe character traits include strong, weak, polite, rude, selfish, selfless, prejudiced, and open-minded, for example. The author develops these traits by telling what the character says, does, and thinks. Writers usually base their characters at least in part on a real person or persons, and then elaborate. (Theodore Taylor was a seaman on a gasoline tanker and then a naval officer during World War II.) A good writer will make the characters believable for the readers.

Explain that this is a "coming-of-age" story, or bildungsroman, where the central character becomes more aware of himself because of events that occur. In this novel, the awareness comes because of Phillip's experiences of blindness and survival on the cay.

Have students look for the character traits of both Phillip and Timothy as they read. Distribute copies of the Character Trait Chart (included.) Ask students to fill in what they have learned about Phillip and Timothy so far. Tell them they should continue to be aware the character traits of both characters as they read, and that they will continue the discussion and complete more of the chart during Lesson 17.

CHARACTER TRAITS CHART *The Cay*

Directions: Fill in the charts fo Phillip and Timothy with examples from the novel.

Phillip's Character Traits	Words, Thoughts, or Actions That Illustrate the Trait
1.	
2.	
3.	

Timothy's Character Traits	Words, Thoughts, or Actions That Illustrate the Trait
1.	
2.	
3.	

LESSON FIVE

Objectives
1. To practice writing to inform
2. To evaluate students' writing skills

Activity #1

Distribute Writing Assignment #1 and discuss the directions in detail. Allow the remaining class time for students to work on the assignment. Give students an additional two or three days to complete the assignment if necessary. FYI Link www.foremostboaters.com/safety/abandon_ship.htm

Activity #2

Distribute copies of the Writing Evaluation Form (included in this Unit Plan.) Explain to the students that during Lesson Nine you will be holding individual writing conferences about this writing assignment. Make sure they are familiar with the criteria on the Writing Evaluation Form.

Follow-Up: After you have graded the assignments, have a writing conference with each student. (This Unit Plan schedules one in Lesson Nine.) After the writing conference, allow students to revise their papers using your suggestions to complete the revisions. You may want to grade the revisions on an A-C-E scale, (all revisions well done, some revisions made, few or no revisions made.) This will speed the grading time and still give some credit for the students' efforts.

LESSON SIX

Objectives
1. To review the main ideas and events in Chapters 6-9
2. To complete the pre-reading and vocabulary work for Chapters 10-12
3. To read Chapters 10-12 silently

Activity #1

Review the study guide questions and answers with students. Then have students work in groups of three or four to write a few additional questions about the chapters. Have each group read their questions aloud and let them call on students to answer the questions.

Activity #2

Give students about fifteen minutes to do the pre-reading and vocabulary work for Chapters 10-12.

Activity #3

Give students the remainder of the period to begin silently reading Chapters 10-12. Remind them that the reading must be completed prior to the next class meeting.

WRITING ASSIGNMENT 1 *The Cay*
Writing to Inform

PROMPT

In chapter 3 you read that the *SS Hato* was torpedoed by a German submarine. The passengers and crew had to abandon ship. Phillip says that the officers had held daily drills for this emergency. Your assignment is to write instructions for abandoning a ship in case of an emergency. You should assume that the ship is the size of the *SS Hato*, or larger.

PREWRITING

In order to be accurate, you will have to do some research on ships and disasters that occur at sea. Your school or public library will have books, newspaper articles, and possibly videos having to do with ships and ship disasters. You may also want to contact the United States Coast Guard or Navy, a cruise line, or a local boat facility for information.

DRAFTING

First, write a paragraph in which you explain why it is necessary to have evacuation procedures and practices on a ship. Use accurate terminology when talking about locations and parts of a ship. You may want to give examples of times when ships had to be abandoned.

In the body of your text, explain how to abandon a sinking or damaged ship. You may find it easier to use a list format here instead of paragraphs. Give information on when to leave the ship, where to go, how to leave, and what to bring with you. If you find information in your research about what to wear or not wear, include that as well.

Finally, write a concluding paragraph that tells again why a ship might need to be abandoned, and why your readers/viewers should obey the advice given by the professionals.

PEER EDITING

When you finish the rough draft of your text, ask another student to read it. After reading your rough draft, the student should tell you what he/she liked best about the work, which parts were difficult to understand, and ways in which your work could be improved. Reread your text considering your critic's comments, and make the revisions you think are necessary.

PROOFREADING

Do a final proofreading of your text, double-checking your grammar, spelling, organization, and the clarity of your ideas.

WRITING EVALUATION FORM *The Cay*

Name _____ Date _____ Class _____

Writing Assignment # _____

Circle One For Each Item:

Composition	excellent	good	fair	poor
Style	excellent	good	fair	poor
Grammar	excellent	good	fair	poor (errors noted)
Spelling	excellent	good	fair	poor (errors noted)
Punctuation	excellent	good	fair	poor (errors noted)
Legibility	excellent	good	fair	poor (errors noted)

Strengths:

Weaknesses:

Comments/Suggestions:

LESSON SEVEN

Objectives
1. To review the main ideas and events in Chapters 10-12
2. To complete the vocabulary and pre-reading work for Chapters 13-15
3. To read Chapters 13-15

Activity #1
Review the study guide questions and answers for Chapters 10-12.

Activity #2
Give students about fifteen minutes to complete the pre-reading and vocabulary work for Chapters 13-15. Allow students to work with partners if they wish to do so.

Activity #3
Depending on the needs of the students, have them read these chapters orally or silently. Remind them that any reading not completed in class must be finished before the next class meeting.

LESSON EIGHT

Objectives
1. To take a quiz on the required reading
2. To become acquainted with Writing Assignment #2

Activity #1
Give students a pop quiz on chapters 13-15. Use either the short answer or multiple choice form of the study guide questions as a quiz so that in discussing the answers to the quiz you also answer the study guide questions. Collect the papers for grading.

Activity #2
Distribute Writing Assignment #2. Discuss the directions in detail and give students ample time to complete the assignment.

WRITING ASSIGNMENT #2 *The Cay*
Writing to Persuade

PROMPT
The *SS Hato* was torpedoed on April 6, 1942. Phillip was found on August 20, 1942. At some point during that time, Phillip had been officially reported lost at sea. The book does not tell the reader anything about the length or intensity of searches that were done to find Phillip and Timothy. Since a war was going on, there might not have been enough resources for a lengthy search. A group of family members and friends of the two victims wants the government to keep searching. They have asked you to present their request for an extended search to the government. You are now preparing that request, and will present it at the next government meeting.

PREWRITING
Make a list of the reasons you and your group want the search to continue. Think of statements to support each of your reasons, and list them under each reason. Then number the reasons in order from most to least important.

DRAFTING
Make an introductory statement in which you describe Phillip, the reason he was sailing to Florida, and your knowledge of what happened. Next describe Timothy and the reasons he was on the ship. Then briefly outline what has been done so far to find the two missing people. Next, state your request.

Write one paragraph for each of your reasons. Use the supporting statements for each reason.

Summarize your request and respectfully ask for a reply from the government by a certain date, possibly a week after the meeting.

PEER CONFERENCING/REVISING
When you finish the rough draft, ask another student to look at it. You may want to give the student your checklist so he/she can double check for you and see that you have included all of the information. After reading, he or she should tell you what he/she liked best about your persuasive speech, which parts were difficult to understand or needed more information, and ways in which your work could be improved. Reread your persuasive speech considering your critic's comments and make the corrections you think are necessary.

PROOFREADING/EDITING
Do a final proofreading of your persuasive speech, double-checking your grammar, spelling, organization, and the clarity of your ideas.

FINAL DRAFT
Follow your teacher's guidelines for completing the final draft of your paper.

LESSON NINE

Student Objectives
    1. To participate in a writing conference with the teacher
    2. To revise Writing Assignment #1 based on the teacher's suggestions

Activity #1
    Call students individually to your desk or some other private area of the classroom. Discuss their papers from Writing Assignment #1. Use the completed Writing Evaluation form as a basis for your critique.

Activity #2
    Students should use this class time (when they are not in conference with you) to work on their non-fiction reading assignment, revisions of Writing Assignment #1, or to review the study guide questions and pre-reading vocabulary worksheets they have completed so far.

LESSON TEN

Objectives
    1. To preview the study questions and vocabulary for chapters 16-19
    2. To read chapters 16-19
    3. To review the main ideas and events from chapters 16-19
    4. To make sure the students have all the answers to all of the previous study guide questions

Activity #1
    Give students about fifteen minutes to complete the pre-reading and vocabulary work for chapters 16-19.

Activity #2
    Have students read the chapters silently and answer the study guide questions.

Activity #3
    Discuss the study guide questions and answers for chapters 16-19.

Activity #4
    Give students time to go through their study guides and notes to see if they are missing any information. Let them work with partners or in small groups to fill in the gaps. Be available for private consultations.

LESSON ELEVEN

Objective
   To discuss *The Cay* at the interpretive and critical levels

Activity #1
   Choose the questions from the Extra Writing Assignments/Discussion Questions which seem most appropriate for your students. A class discussion of these questions is most effective if students have been given the opportunity to formulate answers to the questions prior to the discussion. To this end, you may either have all the students formulate answers to all the questions, divide the class into groups, and assign one or more questions to each group, or you could assign one question to each student in your class. The option you choose will make a difference in the amount of class time needed for this activity.

Activity #2
   After students have had ample time to formulate answers to the questions, begin your class discussion of the questions and the ideas presented by the questions. Be sure students take notes during the discussion so they have information to study for the unit test.

LESSON TWELVE

Objective
   To practice expressing personal opinions in writing

Activity #1
   Write the word *opinion* on the board and ask students what it means. Invite them to give their opinions on topics such as what should be served for lunch in the school cafeteria, if the school should have a dress code, their favorite singer/group. Ask other students to agree or disagree, and state their reasons. Make the point that all people have opinions. A person expressing an opinion should be able to back it up with facts and reasons why he/she has the opinion.

Activity #2
   Distribute copies of Writing Assignment #3. Discuss the assignment in detail with the students. Tell them they will have the remainder of the class period to begin working on the assignment. Give the due date for the completed assignment. It should be a few days before the test.

EXTRA WRITING ASSIGNMENT/DISCUSSION QUESTIONS
The Cay

Interpretive
1. From what point of view is the novel written? How does this affect your understanding of the story?
2. What are the main conflicts in the story? How are they resolved?
3. How important is the setting to the story?
4. How did Phillip change over the course of the novel? Were the changes for the good?
5. What was the overall mood of the story? Give examples to support your answer.
6. Was the use of dialect effective in the novel?
7. What was the high point of the story?
8. Is the story believable? Why or why not?

Critical
9. Compare and contrast Timothy and Phillip.
10. Why did Phillip ask Timothy if he was still black? Why did Timothy laugh?
11. What was Stew Cat's role in the story?
12. Phillip's parents made the decision that Phillip and his mother would travel, even though they knew it was dangerous. What does this tell about them?
13. Is Phillip's physical blindness a metaphor for something else? If so, what is it?
14. Discuss the theme of overcoming prejudice as it is presented in the novel.
15. Discuss Phillip's emergence as a person, and the roles that his mother, father, and Timothy had in his development.
16. Why is the hurricane an important element in the story?
17. Why did Timothy die? What purpose did his death serve in novel?
18. Is the war an important part of the story? If so, what does it contribute? If not, why was it included?

Critical/Personal Response
19. The story does not explain how Phillip's parents felt about his disappearance, or what they did to find him. Does this lack of explanation affect your enjoyment of the story? Why or why not?
20. Phillip had several tragic or difficult circumstances. List as many as you can recall. Which was the hardest, and why?
21. Suppose Phillip had not been blinded. How might the story have changed?
22. Do you think Timothy and Phillip did everything they could to protect themselves from the hurricane? What, if anything, else could they have done to protect themselves?

The Cay Extra Writing Assignments/Discussion Questions Continued

Personal Response

23. Did you enjoy reading The Cay? Why or why not?
24. Would more background information about the war, the islands, Timothy or Phillip have made the story better? Why or why not?
25. Which of the characters did you like, and why? Which did you dislike, and why?
26. How do you think Phillip's parents felt when they found out he was missing?
27. At first, Phillip blamed his troubles on his mother. How might he have felt when he finally got home?
28. Which scene in the story did you like most? Why?
29. What do you think Phillip will do next?
30. Before you read the story, did you think it would be possible to survive on a small tropical island? What do you think after reading the story?
31. Did Phillip's experiences change the way you look at yourself? How?
32. Did you like the ending of the novel? Why or why not? How would you change it?
33. Have you read any other stories similar to *The Cay?* If so, tell about them.
34. Would you recommend this book to another student? Why or why not?
35. Theodore Taylor wrote a prequel-sequel to *The Cay*. It is called *Timothy of the Cay*. Do you think you might read it? Why or why not?

QUOTATIONS *The Cay*
Discuss the significance of the following quotations from the novel.

1. "Like silent, hungry sharks that swim in the darkness of the sea, the German submarines arrived in the middle of the night."

2. "I was not frightened, just terribly excited. War was something I'd heard a lot about, but had never seen."

3. "Where have you been?" "Punda," I admitted. "I went with Henrik."

4. "There's no place nice and safe right now."

5. "Well, then Phillip and I must go back. We'll go back to Norfolk and wait until the danger is over."

6. "There's more danger in the trip back, unless you go by air, than there is in staying here. If they do shell us, they won't hit Scharloo."

7. Just as we were ready to go, there was an explosion and we looked toward the sea. The *Empire Tern* had vanished in a wall of red flames, and black smoke was beginning to boil into the sky. Someone screamed, 'There it is.' We looked off to one side of the flames, about a mile away, and saw a black shape in the water, very low. It was a German submarine, surfaced now to watch the ship die."

8. "I was no longer excited about the war; I had begun to understand that it meant death and destruction."

9. "Your father has finally secured passage for us, so today will be your last day in school here, Phillip. We'll start packing tomorrow, and on Friday, we leave aboard a ship for Miami. Then we'll take the train to Norfolk."

10. "Well, you can rest easy, Phillip. The Germans would never waste a torpedo on this old tub."

11. "He came up beside me, holding my head in his great clamshell hands. It didn't matter, at that moment, that he was black and ugly."

12. "Do not be despair, young bahss. Someone will fin' us. Many schooner go by dis way, an' dis also be d'ship track to Jamaica, an' on."

13. "They are not the same as you, Phillip. They are different and they live differently. That's the way it must be."

The Cay Quotations Continued

14. "I wouldn't even be here with you if it wasn't for my mother." "She started dis terrible wahr, eh, young bahss?"

15. "What do we have to do?" . . . "Stay alive, young bahss, dat's what we 'ave to do."

16. "I'm blind, I'm blind."

17. "I don't want to go on that island." . . . "We be goin' on dat islan', young bahss. Dat be true." . . . "From dis islan', we will get help. Be true, I swear. . . "

18. "True, but we cannot fret 'bout it, can we? We'll make camp, an' see what 'appens."

19. "He was very old. Old enough to die there."

20. "You ugly black man! I won't do it! You're stupid, you can't even spell . . . "

21. "I want to be your friend." . . . "Young bahss, you'ave always been my friend."

22. "I don' like some white people my own self, but 'twould be outrageous if I didn' like any o' dem."

23. "Why b'feesh different color, or flower b'different color? I true don' know, Phill-eep, but I true tink beneath d'skin is all d'same."

24. "You see, Phill-eep, you do not need d'eye now. You 'ave done widout d'eye what I couldn't do wid my whole body."

25. "Timothy, are you still black?"

26. "Why didn't you take us with you?"

27. "Are you all right?"

28. "Son, get some sleep. The *Hato* was sunk way back in April."

29. "Phillip, I'm sorry, I'm so sorry."

30. "Dis b'dat outrageous cay, eh, Timothy?"

WRITING ASSIGNMENT #3 *The Cay*
Personal Opinion

PROMPT
Phillip's parents argued about whether or not he and his mother should go back to Virginia. His father said that if they went, it should be by airplane. His mother said she was afraid to fly; she wanted to go to Miami by boat and then to Norfolk by train. His father felt it was not safe to be on a ship because of the danger from the German submarines. He thought they were safer on the island. Phillip wanted to stay with his father.

Suppose the Enright family came to you to ask your opinion about what to do. They say they will accept your opinion and do whatever you suggest.

PREWRITING
You may want to become an "expert" by reading more about the air and sea strikes during World War II. Also find out more about the situation in Curaçao and the surrounding area. If possible, interview someone who has been in a similar situation as the Enrights. Then form your opinion. Next, brainstorm a list of reasons for your opinion. Decide on the best order for your reasons, and number them on your list.

Hint: Pretend you have not yet read *The Cay*, so you don't know the result of the family's decision. You need to form your opinion based on the information given in the first two chapters of the novel.

DRAFTING
Your opening statement should state the topic and give your opinion about it. Next state your most important reason. Explain your reason with personal experiences or facts about the topic. In the next paragraph, state your next reason and the facts that support it. Write one paragraph for each reason. In your closing paragraph, state your topic and opinion again.

PEER CONFERENCE/REVISING
When you finish the rough draft, ask another student to look at it. You may want to give the student your brainstorm list so he/she can double check for you and see that you have included all of the information. After reading, he or she should tell you what he/she liked best about your opinion paper, which parts were difficult to understand or needed more information, and ways in which your work could be improved. Reread your opinion paper considering your critic's comments and make the corrections you think are necessary.

PROOFREADING/EDITING
Do a final proofreading of your opinion paper, double-checking your grammar, spelling, organization, and the clarity of your ideas.

FINAL DRAFT
Follow your teacher's directions for making a final copy of your paper.

LESSON THIRTEEN

Objectives
1. To conduct library research for the Non-fiction Reading Assignment
2. To complete any unfinished assignments

Activity #1

Take the students to the library/media center for the entire class period. Tell them they can have the time to work on their Non-fiction Reading Assignment. Provide guidance in finding and using resources as necessary. Students who have completed the assignment can complete other unfinished assignments related to the novel unit, or they can use the time to read for pleasure.

LESSON FOURTEEN

Objectives
   1. To listen to the audio book version of *The Cay*
   2. To compare the text and audio versions of *The Cay*

Activity #1

There are several audiocassette versions of The Cay. The running time for the unabridged version is 165 minutes. This may be too long for you to play the entire audiobook in one class setting. If so, you may want to preview the audiobook and choose sections to play for the class.

Be sure to play one of the sections with a lot of dialogue between Phillip and Timothy so students can hear Timothy's speech patterns.

Activity #2

After students listen to the audio version of *The Cay*, invite them to share their reactions to it. The following questions will help spark a discussion.
   1. Which did you prefer, reading or listening?
   2. Did the sound effects in the audio version increase or decrease your enjoyment of the book? Why?
   3. If you listened to an abridged version of the book, was the abridgement effective?
   4. If you had to abridge the book for an audio version, which scenes would you leave out? Why?

Activity #3

Students may enjoy listening to the audio book again in their free time, or reading along with some chapters.

Note: In 1974 Universal Films made a movie of *The Cay* starring James Earl Jones. This movie may still be available from libraries or video stores that stock old films. It is not in current circulation.

LESSON FIFTEEN

Objectives
    1. To widen the breadth of students' knowledge about the topics discussed or touched upon in *The Cay*
    2. To present the nonfiction assignments

Activity #1

    Ask each student to give a brief oral report about the nonfiction work he/she read for the nonfiction assignment. Your criteria for evaluating this report will vary depending on the level of your students. You may wish for students to give the complete report without using notes of any kind. Or you may want students to read directly from a written report. You may want to do something between these two options. Make students aware of your criteria in ample time for them to prepare their reports.

    Start with one student's report. After that, ask if anyone else in the class has read on a topic related to the first student's report. If no one has, choose another student at random. After each report, be sure to ask if anyone has a report related to the one just completed. That will help keep continuity during the discussion of the reports.

Activity #2

    Collect the students' written reports. Put them in a binder and have the binder available for students to read.

Activity #3

    If the class or school has a Web site, post the nonfiction reports there.

LESSON SIXTEEN

<u>Objective</u>

To review all of the vocabulary work done in this unit

VOCABULARY REVIEW ACTIVITIES

1. Divide your class into two teams and have an old-fashioned spelling or definition bee.

2. Give individuals or groups of students a *The Cay* Vocabulary Word Search Puzzle with a word list. The person (group) to find all of the vocabulary words in the puzzle first wins.

3. Give students a *The Cay* Vocabulary Word Search Puzzle without the word list. The person or group to find the most vocabulary words in the puzzle wins.

4. Put a *The Cay* Vocabulary Crossword Puzzle onto a transparency on the overhead projector and do the puzzle together as a class.

5. Give students a *The Cay* Vocabulary Matching Worksheet to do.

6. Use words from the word jumble page and have students spell them correctly, then use them in original sentences.

7. Play Vocabulary Bingo with the materials enclosed with this unit. The Caller calls out definitions for the vocabulary words. If a student has that word on his/her card, that word is covered with a piece of paper. When someone gets a column, row, or diagonal filled-in he/she yells out, "Bingo!" and wins that round.

8. Have students write a story in which they correctly use as many vocabulary words as possible. Have students read their compositions orally. Post the most original compositions on your bulletin board.

9. Have students work in teams and play charades with the vocabulary words.

10. Select a word of the day and encourage students to use it correctly in their writing and speaking vocabulary.

11. Have a contest to see which students can find the most vocabulary words used in other sources. You may want to have a bulletin board available so the students can write down their word, the sentence it was used in, and the source.

LESSON SEVENTEEN

Objective
    To review the main ideas presented in *The Cay*

Activity #1
    Choose one of the review games/activities included in the packet and spend your class period as outlined there.

Activity #2
    Remind students of the date for the Unit Test. Stress the review of the Study Guides and their class notes as a last minute, brush-up review for homework.

REVIEW GAMES / ACTIVITIES

1. Ask the class to make up a unit test for *The Cay*. The test should have 4 sections: multiple choice, true/false, short answer and essay. Students may use 1/2 period to make the test, including a separate answer sheet, and then swap papers and use the other 1/2 class period to take a test a classmate has devised. (open book)

2. Take 1/2 period for students to make up true and false questions (including the answers). Collect the papers and divide the class into two teams. Draw a big tic-tac-toe board on the chalkboard. Make one team X and one team O. Ask questions to each side, giving each student one turn. If the question is answered correctly, that student's team's letter (X or O) is placed in the box. If the answer is incorrect, no mark is placed in the box. The object is to get three marks in a row like tic-tac-toe. You may want to keep track of the number of games won for each team.

3. Take 1/2 period for students to make up questions (true/false and short answer). Collect the questions. Divide the class into two teams. You'll alternate asking questions to individual members of teams A & B (like in a spelling bee). The question keeps going from A to B until it is correctly answered, then a new question is asked. A correct answer does not allow the team to get another question. Correct answers are +2 points; incorrect answers are -1 point.

4. Allow students time to quiz each other (in pairs) from their study guides and class notes.

5. Give students a *The Cay* crossword puzzle to complete.

6. Play *The Cay* bingo using the materials included with this unit. The Caller gives clues to which the students must know the one-word answer. If that answer appears on their cards, they place a piece of paper over that word. The first student to have a filled-in row, column, or diagonal (like bingo) wins! (You should have students call off their filled-in words to make sure that all of their responses were correct).

7. Divide your class into two teams. Use the *Hatchet* crossword words with their letters jumbled as a word list. Student 1 from Team A faces off against Student 1 from Team B. You write the first jumbled word on the board. The first student (1A or 1B) to unscramble the word wins the chance for his/her team to score points. If 1A wins the jumble, go to student 2A and give him/her a clue. He/she must give you the correct word which matches that clue. If he/she does, Team A scores a point, and you give student 3A a clue for which you expect another correct response. Continue giving Team A clues until some team member makes an incorrect response. An incorrect response sends the game back to the jumbled-word face off, this time with students 2A and 2B. Instead of repeating giving clues to the first few students of each team, continue with the student after the one who gave the last incorrect response on the team.

8. Take on the persona of "The Answer Person." Allow students to ask any question about the book. Answer the questions, or tell students where to look in the book to find the answer.

9. Students may enjoy playing charades with events from the story. Select a student to start. Give him/her a card with a scene or event from the story. Allow the players to use their books to find the scene being described. The first person to guess each charade performs the next one.

10. Play a categories-type quiz game. (A master is included in this Unit Plan). Make an overhead transparency of the categories form. Divide the class into teams of three or four players each. Have each team Choose a recorder and a banker. Choose a team to go first. That team will choose a category and point amount. Ask the question to the entire class.(Use the Study Guide Quiz and Vocabulary questions.) Give the teams one minute to discuss the answer and write it down. Walk around the room and check the answers. Each team that answers correctly receives the points. (Incorrect answers are not penalized; they just don't receive any points). Cross out that square on the playing board. Play continues until all squares have been used. The winning team is the one with the most points. You can assign bonus points to any square or squares you choose.

11. Have individual students draw scenes from the book. Display the scenes and have the rest of the class look in their books to find the chapter or section that is being depicted. The first student to find the correct scene then displays his or her picture. When the game is over, collect the pictures and put them in a binder for students to look at during their free time.

NOTE: If students do not need the extra review, omit this lesson and go on to the test.

QUIZ GAME *The Cay*

Chapters 1-3	Chapters 4-7	Chapters 8-11	Chapters 12-15	Chapters 16-Epilogue
100	100	100	100	100
200	200	200	200	200
300	300	300	300	300
400	400	400	400	400
500	500	500	500	500

LESSON EIGHTEEN

Objective
> To test the students' understanding of the main ideas and themes in The Cay

Activity #1
> Distribute the *The Cay* Unit Tests. Go over the instructions in detail and allow the students the entire class period to complete the exam.

Activity #2
> Collect all test papers and assigned books prior to the end of the class period.

NOTES ABOUT THE UNIT TESTS IN THIS UNIT:

There are 5 different unit tests which follow.

There are two short answer tests which are based primarily on facts from the novel. The answer key for short answer unit test 1 follows the student test. The answer key for short answer test 2 follows the student short answer unit test 2.

There is one advanced short answer unit test. It is based on the extra discussion questions. Use the matching key for short answer unit test 2 to check the matching section of the advanced short answer unit test. There is no key for the short answer questions. The answers will be based on the discussions you have had during class.

There are two multiple choice unit tests. Following the two unit tests, you will find an answer sheet on which students should mark their answers. The same answer sheet should be used for both tests; however, students' answers will be different for each test. Following the students' answer sheet for the multiple choice tests you will find your two keys: one for multiple choice test 1 and one for multiple choice test 2.

The short answer tests have a vocabulary section. You should choose 10 of the vocabulary words from this unit, read them orally and have the students write them down. Then, either have students write a definition or use the words in sentences. The second part of the vocabulary test is matching.

UNIT TESTS

SHORT ANSWER UNIT TEST 1 *The Cay*

I. Matching/Identify

Directions: Place the letter of the matching definition on the blank line.

_____ 1. Curaçao   A. wanted to return to Norfolk

_____ 2. *SS Empire Tern*   B. wanted to head for land

_____ 3. Willemstad   C. thought they should stay where they were

_____ 4. Phillip   D. Timothy's birthplace

_____ 5. Timothy   E. tanker that was torpedoed by the Germans

_____ 6. *SS Hato*   F. group of islands cut off by a coral reef

_____ 7. Mrs. Enright   G. had to be abandoned after being torpedoed

_____ 8. Mr. Enright   H. city where the Enrights lived

_____ 9. Charlotte Amalie   I. wanted to stay on the water

_____ 10. Devil's Mouth   J. Dutch oil-producing island

II. Short Answer

Directions: Answer each question with details from the novel.

1. Describe the conflict between Mr. and Mrs. Enright. Tell how it was resolved.

2. What event occurs just as the story opens? How does this event change life on Curaçao?

Short Answer Unit Test 1 *The Cay*

3. Describe the events that occurred when the SS Hato was torpedoed.

4. How did Phillip feel when he realized he was blind? What did he do?

5. Explain why Phillip fell off the raft into the water. Tell what was in the water. Tell what Timothy did when Phillip fell in.

6. How did Timothy and Phillip feel about leaving the raft?

Short Answer Unit Test 1 *The Cay*

7. Describe the things Timothy did to make the cay more livable. Include the things he did to help Phillip get around the cay.

8. Describe what happened when Phillip lost his temper when Timothy asked him to make the mats. Explain what Phillip's first response was, what he thought about a little later, and what he did about it. What was Timothy's response?

9. Describe the events that took place just before, during, and after the hurricane.

10. Explain how Phillip was finally rescued. Include the date of his rescue, and tell how long he was on the island.

Short Answer Unit Test 1 *The Cay*

III. Quotations

Directions: Identify the speaker and discuss the significance of each of the following quotations.

1. "I was not frightened, just terribly excited. War was something I'd heard a lot about, but had never seen."

2. "I wouldn't even be here with you if it wasn't for my mother." "She started dis terrible wahr, eh, young bahss?"

3. "Timothy, are you still black?"

4. "True, but we cannot fret 'bout it, can we? We'll make camp, an' see what 'appens."

5. "I'm here! I'm here!"

Short Answer Unit Test 1 *The Cay*

IV. Essay

Discuss the changes in Phillip's opinion of black people. Tell his opinion before he spent time on the island with Timothy, and how he got that opinion. Describe how his opinion changed and the events that led to the change.

Short Answer Unit Test 1 *The Cay*

V. Vocabulary Part 1

Listen to the vocabulary word and spell it. After you have spelled all the words, go back and write down the definitions.

WORD	DEFINITION
1. _____	_____
2. _____	_____
3. _____	_____
4. _____	_____
5. _____	_____
6. _____	_____
7. _____	_____
8. _____	_____
9. _____	_____
10. _____	_____

Vocabulary Part 2

Directions: Place the letter of the matching definition on the blank line.

_____ 1. refinery   A. a small, low island
_____ 2. wrenching   B. extreme anxiety
_____ 3. parch   C. a place for processing raw materials such as sugar and oil
_____ 4. cay   D. recurring illness transmitted by mosquitoes
_____ 5. fronds   E. narrow cracks
_____ 6. anguish   F. pulling or twisting away
_____ 7. catchment   G. searched by feeling
_____ 8. malaria   H. large, divided leaves
_____ 9. crevices   I. device for collecting rainwater
_____ 10. Groped   J. dry out

ANSWER KEY SHORT ANSWER UNIT TEST 1 *The Cay*

I. Matching/Identify

Directions: Place the letter of the matching definition on the blank line.

J.	1. Curaçao	A.	wanted to return to Norfolk
E.	2. *SS Empire Tern*	B.	wanted to head for land
H.	3. Willemstad	C.	thought they should stay where they were
I.	4. Phillip	D.	Timothy's birthplace
B.	5. Timothy	E.	tanker that was torpedoed by the Germans
G	6. *SS Hato*	F.	group of cays cut off by a coral reef
A	7. Mrs. Enright	G.	had to be abandoned after being torpedoed
C.	8. Mr. Enright	H.	city where the Enrights lived
D.	9. Charlotte Amalie	I.	wanted to stay on the water
F.	10. Devil's Mouth	J.	Dutch oil-producing island

II. Short Answer

Directions: Answer each question with details from the novel.

1. Describe the conflict between Mr. and Mrs. Enright. Tell how it was resolved.

    Mrs. Enright wanted to take Phillip and return to Norfolk, Virginia. She wanted to go by boat because she was afraid to fly. Mr. Enright thought they were safer where they were living, in Willemstad. He said if they did go, it should be by airplane. Mrs. Enright got her way and took Phillip away from Curaçao by freighter.

2. What event occurs just as the story opens? How does this event change life on Curaçao?

    German submarines attacked the Dutch oil refinery on the island of Aruba. They also attacked six small lake tankers that belonged to the island of Curaçao. After the attack, real soldiers with machine guns and rifles appeared around the Fort Amsterdam. Everyone was tense. Men chased away the boys who liked to play near the fort.

3. Describe the events that occurred when the *SS Hato* was torpedoed.

The *Hato* was torpedoed at 3 A. M. on April 6, 1942, 2 days after leaving Panama. Phillip's mother was calm and helped him put on his lifejacket. The sailors were putting the passengers into the lifeboat. Phillip was being helped in when the *Hato* lurched. The lifeboat tilted and the passengers landed in the water. Something hit Timothy on the head. When he woke up he was on a raft with a black man and a cat.

4. How did Phillip feel when he realized he was blind? What did he do?

Phillip screamed to Timothy, "I'm blind, I'm blind." He touched his eyes and realized that the pain from the headache was gone. He felt frightened and then angry. He began to craw around on the raft, screaming for his parents. Timothy held onto him. Phillip hit Timothy. Timothy let Phillip hit him.

5. Explain why Phillip fell off the raft into the water. Tell what was in the water. Tell what Timothy did when Phillip fell in.

Timothy shouted that he spotted land. Phillip jumped up, and in his excitement he lost his balance and fell overboard. Timothy jumped in and hauled Phillip back onto the raft. He yelled at Phillip to be more careful because of the sharks in the water.

6. How did Timothy and Phillip feel about leaving the raft?

Timothy thought it was a good idea to go to land. He thought they would have a better chance of getting help that way. Phillip wanted to stay on the raft because he thought the Navy was still searching for them.

7. Describe the things Timothy did to make the cay more livable. Include the things he did to help Phillip get around the cay.

He built a signal fire and spelled the word "help" on the beach with stones. He made a hut about 40 feet away from the shore. He wove a rope for Phillip and stretched it from the hut to the beach and signal fire. He caught fish and langosta for them to eat.

8. Describe what happened when Phillip lost his temper when Timothy asked him to make the mats. Explain what Phillip's first response was, what he thought about a little later, and what he did about it. What was Timothy's response?

9. Describe the events that took place just before, during, and after the hurricane.

They heard a sound like a rifle shot. Timothy said it was the waves, warning that a hurricane was coming. He lashed the He lashed the water keg to a palm tree trunk. He tied the rest of the rope around the tree trunk so they could hang onto it if necessary. They ate a large meal. He put his knife in the tin box and lashed the box to the tree.

10. Explain how Phillip was finally rescued. Include the date of his rescue, and tell how long he was shipwrecked.

    Phillip heard a heavy sound that he realized were explosions. He built up the signal fire with more sea grape leaves. The plane got close, but then it left. Then Phillip felt ill and lay down on his mat. A little while later he heard the sound of a bell. He ran to the beach and called, "I'm here! I'm here!" He heard a voice and asked the man to take Stew Cat and lead him to the boat. Then he asked one of the sailors to go back and get Timothy's knife. He was transferred to the destroyer, where he told the captain his name and everything that had happened. The Hato sank on April 6, 1942. Phillip was rescued on August 20, 1942. That is a total of a little over 5 months.

Answer Key Short Answer Unit Test 1 *The Cay*

III. Quotations

Directions: Identify the speaker and discuss the significance of each of the following quotations.

1. "I was not frightened, just terribly excited. War was something I'd heard a lot about, but had never seen."

    Phillip said this near the beginning of the novel. He had just heard the news about the Germans sinking the tankers and destroying the island of Aruba.

2. "I wouldn't even be here with you if it wasn't for my mother." "She started dis terrible wahr, eh, young bahss?"

    Phillip said the first line to Timothy when they were on the raft. This was before he went blind. Timothy replied with the second line.

3. "Timothy, are you still black?"

    Philip said this on a night in late May, as they were lying in their hut. They had talked about many things, including prejudice Timothy had taught him to fish. Phillip had just climbed the coconut tree and realized how much he could do without eyesight. Timothy laughed in response.

4. "True, but we cannot fret 'bout it, can we? We'll make camp, an' see what 'appens."

    They had just landed on the cay. Phillip still had misgivings about going to land. Timothy had told Phillip that he thought they were in an area called The Devil's Mouth. Phillip was concerned that aircraft would see their signal fire but think it was local fishermen.

5. "I'm here! I'm here!"

    Phillip had heard an airplane and built up the signal fire with oily sea grape leaves to make black smoke. The plane went over but did not land. A little while later he heard a bell ringing. He ran to the beach and shouted to the men in the boat.

V. Vocabulary Part 1
   Choose 10 words. List them here with their definitions as a key if you choose to do so.

WORD   **DEFINITION**

1. _____   _____

2. _____   _____

3. _____   _____

4. _____   _____

5. _____   _____

6. _____   _____

7. _____   _____

8. _____   _____

9. _____   _____

10. _____   _____

Vocabulary Part 2
   Directions: Place the letter of the matching definition on the blank line.

C.   1. refinery   A. a small, low island
F   2. wrenching   B. extreme anxiety
J   3. parch   C. a place for processing raw materials such as sugar and oil
A   4. cay   D. recurring illness transmitted by mosquitoes
H   5. fronds   E. narrow cracks
B   6. anguish   F. pulling or twisting away
I   7. catchment   G. searched by feeling
D   8. malaria   H. large, divided leaves
E   9. crevices   I. device for collecting rainwater
G   10. Groped   J. dry out

SHORT ANSWER UNIT TEST 2 *The Cay*

I. Matching/Identify

Directions: Place the letter of the matching definition on the blank line.

_____ 1. Willemstad   A. city where the Enrights lived

_____ 2. Timothy   B. Dutch oil producing island

_____ 3. Devil's Mouth   C. Timothy's home

_____ 4. Curaçao   D. wanted to stay on the water

_____ 5. Phillip   E. thought the family should stay were they were

_____ 6. Charlotte Amalie   F. wanted to return to Norfolk

_____ 7. *SS Hato*   G. tanker torpedoed by the Germans

_____ 8. *SS Empire Tern*   H. had to be abandoned after being torpedoed

_____ 9. Mr. Enright   I. group of cays cut off by a coral reef

_____ 10. Mrs. Enright   J. wanted to head for land

II. Short Answer

Directions: Answer each question with details from the novel.

1. What was Phillip's reaction to his mother telling him they were leaving the island to return to Norfolk?

2. Where were the Enrights from? What were they doing on Curaçao?

Short Answer Unit Test 2 *The Cay*

3. Describe the days Timothy and Phillip spent on the raft. Tell what they did and what they talked about.

4. Explain Phillip's attitude toward Timothy and how and why it changed.

5. Describe the events that took place just before, during, and after the hurricane.

6. Tell what the cay looked like when they landed. Tell how Phillip and Timothy spent their first few weeks on the cay.

Short Answer Unit Test 2 *The Cay*

7. Tell how Phillip survived after Timothy died.

8. What did Phillip say he would like to do some day?

9. Did Phillip's sight ever return? If so, explain when and how this happened.

10. Describe what Phillip did when he returned to Curaçao after being rescued.

Short Answer Unit Test 2 *The Cay*

III. Quotations

Directions: Identify the speaker and discuss the significance of each of the following quotations.

1. "Dis b'dat outrageous cay, eh, Timothy?"

2. "You see, Phill-eep, you do not need d'eye now. You 'ave done widout d'eye what I couldn't do wid my whole body."

3. "He was very old. Old enough to die there."

4. "You ugly black man! I won't do it! You're stupid, you can't even spell . . ."

5. "Well, you can rest easy, Phillip. The Germans would never waste a torpedo on this old tub."

Short Answer Unit Test 2 *The Cay*

IV. Essay

Describe Phillip's growth as a person. Explain the roles that his blindness and Timothy had in influencing his growth.

Short Answer Unit Test 2 *The Cay*

V. Vocabulary Part 1

    Listen to the vocabulary word and spell it. After you have spelled all the words, go back and write down the definitions.

WORD	DEFINITION
1. _____	_____
2. _____	_____
3. _____	_____
4. _____	_____
5. _____	_____
6. _____	_____
7. _____	_____
8. _____	_____
9. _____	_____
10. _____	_____

Vocabulary Part 2

    Directions: Place the letter of the matching definition on the blank line.

_____ 1. honing   A. unusual, suggesting a supernatural connection
_____ 2. idling   B. low, humming sound
_____ 3. eerie   C. brownish black color
_____ 4. unraveled   D. sharpening
_____ 5. tethered   E. white mineral used for decorative plaster work
_____ 6. drone   F. away from the wind
_____ 7. fret   G. tied to
_____ 8. alabaster   H. took apart; unwound
_____ 9. ebony   I. operating, but not in gear
_____ 10. leeward   J. worry

ANSWER KEY SHORT ANSWER UNIT TEST 2 *The Cay*

I. Matching/Identify

Directions: Place the letter of the matching definition on the blank line.

A.	1. Willemstad	A.	city where the Enrights lived
J	2. Timothy	B.	Dutch oil producing island
I	3. Devil's Mouth	C.	Timothy's home
B	4. Curaçao	D.	wanted to stay on the water
D	5. Phillip	E.	thought the family should stay were they were
C	6. Charlotte Amalie	F.	wanted to return to Norfolk
H	7. *SS Hato*	G.	tanker torpedoed by the Germans
G	8. *SS Empire Tern*	H.	had to be abandoned after being torpedoed
E	9. Mr. Enright	I.	group of cays cut off by a coral reef
F	10. Mrs. Enright	J.	wanted to head for land

II. Short Answer

Directions: Answer each question with details from the novel.

1. What was Phillip's reaction to his mother telling him they were leaving the island to return to Norfolk?

    He felt hollow inside. He became angry and told his mother she was a coward. He said he hated her.

2. Where were the Enrights from? What were they doing on Curaçao?

    They were from Norfolk, Virginia. Mr. Enright had been in charge of building a new oil refinery there. In 1939 the Royal Dutch Shell company had asked the American company if Mr. Enright could help them on Curaçao because he was an expert in refineries and gasoline production.

Answer Key Short Answer Unit Test 2 *The Cay*

3. Describe the days Timothy and Phillip spent on the raft. Tell what they did and what they talked about.

   Phillip woke up about 4 hours after Timothy pulled him from the water. Timothy explained that Phillip had been hit on the head with something when the *Hato* lurched. At first Phillip cried and screamed for his parents. Then he settled down. Timothy ripped a few boards from the sides of the raft and made a small shelter with them. He rationed the water and caught a fe flying fish for them to eat. The next day he went blind. On the third day they heard a motor and Timothy made a signal flare, but no one rescued them. On the fourth day they saw the cay. Timothy wanted to land but Phillip wanted to stay on the water. They drifted toward the cay and Timothy landed the raft on the beach.

4. Explain Phillip's attitude toward Timothy and how and why it changed.

   Phillip had seen black people but had never been very close to them. His mother had told him that black people were different. At first Phillip thought Timothy was ugly. Even though his parents had told him to address older men as "Mister" he did not think Timothy was a mister. Phillip did not want to get physically close to Timothy, but gradually this changed. Phillip realized that Timothy was doing things to make both of their lives better. One night they talked about skin color. Timothy said he thought all people were the same on the inside. After a while Phillip's memory of Timothy's face changed from ugly to kind and strong.

5. Describe the events that took place just before, during, and after the hurricane.

   They heard a sound like a rifle shot. Timothy said it was the waves, warning that a hurricane was coming. He lashed the He lashed the water keg to a palm tree trunk. He tied the rest of the rope around the tree trunk so they could hang onto it if necessary. They ate a large meal. He put his knife in the tin box and lashed the box to the tree. The wind blew the hut away so they lay flat on the ground for two hours. Then Timothy roped Phillip to the tree and put himself at Phillip's back so that his own back was facing the wind. The water rose to their knees and crashed against them. They were both knocked unconscious. When Phillip woke up, he moved Timothy to the ground. Timothy's back had been severely cut by the blowing sand and rain. They both slept. When Phillip woke up, Timothy was dead. Phillip cried for a long time. That afternoon, he buried Timothy.

6. Tell what the cay looked like when they landed. Tell how Phillip and Timothy spent their first few weeks on the cay.

   It was melon shaped, about a mile long and a half-mile wide. There were lizards, sea grape vines, and a few palm trees. There was a small rise about forty feet from the shore. Timothy used palm fronds to build a hut. He built a signal fire on the beach and a smaller fire near the hut. He made a rope from vines and stretched it from the hut to the signal fire and the beach. He made a cane so Phillip could feel his way along. Timothy fished and caught langostas for food.

Answer Key Short Answer Unit Test 2 *The Cay*

7. Tell how Phillip survived after Timothy died.

He buried Timothy near the last palm tree and said a prayer. Then he found the water keg and the tin box. He cleaned up the camp area and put palm fronds and driftwood in separate piles. He used palm fronds to make a bed. He found the fishing poles and honed Timothy's knife. He found another can and began putting a pebble in every day to keep track of the time. Phillip dove into the fishing hole once, but something in there bit him. After that he stayed out.

8. What did Phillip say he would like to do some day?

He would like to take a boat from Panama and find the cay. Then he would visit Timothy's grave.

9. Did Phillip's sight ever return? If so, explain when and how this happened.

Yes, his parents took him to a hospital in New York City. He had three operations and his sight returned. However, he had to wear glasses from then on.

10. Describe what Phillip did when he returned to Curaçao after being rescued.

He spent some time with his friend Henrik, but their friendship wasn't the same as it had been before the war. He visited St. Anna Bay and the Ruyterkade market, where he talked to black people. Some of them had known Timothy. He looked at charts of the Caribbean islands, and found the Devil's mouth.

Answer Key Short Answer Unit Test 2 *The Cay*

III. Quotations
Directions: Identify the speaker and discuss the significance of each of the following quotations.

1. "Dis b'dat outrageous cay, eh, Timothy?"
    At the end of the story, Phillip said he wanted to find the cay someday. When he did, he would stand at Timothy's grave and say that greeting to him.

2. "You see, Phill-eep, you do not need d'eye now. You 'ave done widout d'eye what I couldn't do wid my whole body."
    Phillip had successfully climbed the palm tree and brought down two coconuts for them to eat.

3. "He was very old. Old enough to die there."
    Phillip had asked Timothy his age, and Timothy had replied that he was more than seventy years old. Phillip was concerned that Timothy might die and leave him alone on the island.

4. "You ugly black man! I won't do it! You're stupid, you can't even spell . . . "
    Timothy had asked Phillip to weave their sleeping mats from palm fibers. Phillip tried but was not successful. He threw the fibers at Timothy and yelled. He made the comment about spelling because earlier, Timothy had wanted to use stones on the beach to spell "help." Since he did not know how to spell, Phillip placed the rocks. Phillip felt superior to Timothy.

5. "Well, you can rest easy, Phillip. The Germans would never waste a torpedo on this old tub."
    Mr. Enright said this when he accompanied his wife and son onto the *SS Hato*. Even though he tried to make it sound like a joke, Phillip watched his father check the fire hoses and lifeboats. He looked worried.

Answer Key Short Answer Unit Test 2 *The Cay*

V. Vocabulary Part 1

Choose 10 vocabulary words. Write them here with their definitions if you choose.

WORD **DEFINITION**

1. _____ _____
2. _____ _____
3. _____ _____
4. _____ _____
5. _____ _____
6. _____ _____
7. _____ _____
8. _____ _____
9. _____ _____
10. _____ _____

Vocabulary Part 2

Directions: Place the letter of the matching definition on the blank line.

D.	1. honing	A. unusual, suggesting a supernatural connection
I.	2. idling	B. low, humming sound
A.	3. eerie	C. brownish black color
H.	4. unraveled	D. sharpening
G.	5. tethered	E. white mineral used for decorative plaster work
B.	6. drone	F. away from the wind
J.	7. fret	G. tied to
E.	8. alabaster	H. took apart; unwound
C.	9. ebony	I. operating, but not in gear
F.	10. leeward	J. worry

ADVANCED SHORT ANSWER UNIT TEST *The Cay*

<u>I. Matching/Identify</u>

Directions: Place the letter of the matching definition on the blank line.

_____ 1. Willemstad   A. city where the Enrights lived

_____ 2. Timothy   B. Dutch oil producing island

_____ 3. Devil's Mouth   C. Timothy's home

_____ 4. Curaçao   D. wanted to stay on the water

_____ 5. Phillip   E. thought the family should stay were they were

_____ 6. Charlotte Amalie F. wanted to return to Norfolk

_____ 7. *SS Hato*   G. tanker torpedoed by the Germans

_____ 8. *SS Empire Tern* H. had to be abandoned after being torpedoed

_____ 9. Mr. Enright   I. group of cays cut off by a coral reef

_____ 10. Mrs. Enright   J. wanted to head for land

<u>II. Short Answer</u>

1. Discuss the changes in Phillip's opinion of black people. Tell his opinion before he spent time on the island with Timothy, and how he got that opinion. Describe how his opinion changed, and the events that led to the change.

Advanced Short Answer Unit Test *The Cay*

2. Discuss Phillip's emergence as a person, and the roles that his mother, father, Timothy, and his blindness had in his development.

3. Phillip's parents made a choice for him and his mother to travel, even though they knew it was dangerous. What does this tell about them?

4. Phillip had several tragic or difficult circumstances. Which was the hardest, and why?

5. Is Phillip's physical blindness a metaphor for something else? If so, what is it?

Advanced Short Answer Unit Test *The Cay*

III. Quotations
Directions: Identify the speaker and discuss the significance of each quotation.

1. "You ugly black man! I won't do it! You're stupid, you can't even spell . . . "

2. "Like silent, hungry sharks that swim in the darkness of the sea, the German submarines arrived in the middle of the night."

3. "He came up beside me, holding my head in his great clamshell hands. It didn't matter, at that moment, that he was black and ugly."

4. "Dis b'dat outrageous cay, eh, Timothy?"

5. "When I had fished before, it was fun. Now, I felt I had done something very special. I was learning to do things all over again, by touch and feel."

Advanced Short Answer Unit Test *The Cay*

IV. Vocabulary

Listen to the words and write them down. After you have written down all of the words, write a paragraph in which you use all of the words. The paragraph must in some way relate to *The Cay*.

ANSWER KEY ADVANCED SHORT ANSWER UNIT TEST *The Cay*

I. Matching/Identify

Directions: Place the letter of the matching definition on the blank line.

A.	1. Willemstad	A. city where the Enrights lived
J	2. Timothy	B. Dutch oil producing island
I	3. Devil's Mouth	C. Timothy's home
B	4. Curaçao	D. was rescued from the cay
D	5. Phillip	E. thought the family should stay were they were
C	6. Charlotte Amalie	F. wanted to return to Norfolk
H	7. *SS Hato*	G. tanker torpedoed by the Germans
G	8. *SS Empire Tern*	H. had to be abandoned after being torpedoed
E	9. Mr. Enright	I. group of islands cut off by a coral reef
F	10. Mrs. Enright	J. died on the cay

MULTIPLE CHOICE UNIT TEST 1 *The Cay*

I. Matching/Identify

Directions: Place the letter of the matching definition on the blank line.

_____ 1. Curaçao   A. wanted to return to Norfolk

_____ 2. *SS Empire Tern*   B. died on the cay

_____ 3. Willemstad   C. thought they should stay where they were

_____ 4. Phillip   D. Timothy's birthplace

_____ 5. Timothy   E. tanker that was torpedoed by the Germans

_____ 6. *SS Hato*   F. group of islands cut off by a coral reef

_____ 7. Mrs. Enright   G. had to be abandoned after being torpedoed

_____ 8. Mr. Enright   H. city where the Enrights lived

_____ 9. Charlotte Amalie I. was rescued from the cay

_____ 10. Devil's Mouth   J. Dutch oil-producing island

II. Multiple Choice

1. What was different at the Queen Emma pontoon bridge when Phillip sneaked away to see it?
    A. The bridge was stuck open. No one was trying to fix it.
    B. Soldiers were standing at the entrance to the bridge.
    C. The bridge had been blown up.
    D. Ferryboats and schooners were tied up and empty. Black men were not laughing and shouting.

2. What was the Enright family doing in Curaçao?
    A. Mrs. Enright was teaching school there.
    B. They were on vacation.
    C. Royal Dutch Shell had borrowed Mr. Enright from his regular company for the war effort.
    D. Phillip was an exchange student. His parents had gone there to get him at the end of the term.

Multiple Choice Unit Test 1 *The Cay*

3. What effect did the episode with the *SS Empire Tern* have on Phillip?
    A. He felt pride in the sailors and the ship.
    B. He began to understand that war meant death and destruction.
    C. He feared for his father's life.
    D. He wanted to fight the Germans himself.

4. How did Phillip describe his father as he was standing on the wall of Fort Amsterdam, waving to them on the ship?
    A. a brave and happy man
    B. a tall and lonely figure
    C. an angry and impatient person
    D. an encouraging and strong father

5. Which of the following phrases does **not** describe the man Phillip saw on the raft?
    A. ugly
    B. flat nose and broad face
    C. short and fat
    D. wiry gray hair

6. What items were on the raft that the man on the raft said was "rare good luck"?
    A. There was a keg of water, biscuits, chocolate, and dry matches.
    B. There were signal flares, two blankets, and several teabags.
    C. There was a knife, a can opener, and three cans of tuna.
    D. There were two paddles, a lifejacket, and four oranges.

7. How did Phillip feel when he realized his condition?
    A. frightened and then angry
    B. glad it was not worse
    C. optimistic that he would get better
    D. confused

8. What two things did Timothy do to alert ships to their location?
    A. He built a signal fire and spelled the word "help" on the beach with stones.
    B. He hung a white cloth from one of the palm trees and built a signal fire.
    C. He built a tower of stones and shells and pulled the raft onto the sand.
    D. He spelled the words "save us" on the beach with shells and set fire to the palm trees.

Multiple Choice Unit Test 1 *The Cay*

9. During the hurricane, how were Timothy and Phillip positioned at the palm tree?
    A. They were standing on opposite sides of the tree.
    B. Phillip was high up on the trunk and Timothy was at the base.
    C. They were both up at the top.
    D. Phillip was against the bark and Timothy was up against his back.

10. What did Phillip say about his loss of sight?
    A. His senses of touch and hearing were making up for it.
    B. He did not think he could survive much longer without it.
    C. He thought he would be even lonelier if he could see how deserted he was.
    D. He did not understand why he was being punished this way.

III. Quotations
Identify the speaker:

    A. Phillip   C. Mrs. Enright   E. Mr. Enright
    B. Timothy   D. man from the rescue boat   F. ship's captain

1. "Are you all right?"

2. "You see, Phill-eep, you do not need d'eye now. You 'ave done widout d'eye what I couldn't do wid my whole body."

3. "Well, you can rest easy, Phillip. The Germans would never waste a torpedo on this old tub."

4. "You ugly black man! I won't do it! You're stupid, you can't even spell . . . "

5. "There's no place nice and safe right now."

6. "Son, get some sleep. The *Hato* was sunk way back in April."

7. "Well, then Phillip and I must go back. We'll go back to Norfolk and wait until the danger is over."

8. ". . . . are you still black?"

9. "Dis b'dat outrageous cay, eh, ... ?"

10. They are not the same as you, Phillip. They are different and they live differently. That's the way it must be."

Multiple Choice Unit Test 1 *The Cay*

IV. Vocabulary Matching

1. honing — A. illness transmitted by infected mosquitoes
2. fret — B. stakes
3. dikes — C. tied to
4. distilled — D. sharpening
5. parch — E. extreme anxiety
6. fare — F. went back or further away
7. murmuring — G. stop
8. cay — H. search for something carefully
9. anguish — I. involving hidden dangers or hazards
10. catchment — J. fragments of broken things
11. tethered — K. worry
12. malaria — L. small, low island
13. cease — M. dry out
14. treacherous — N. thin, transparent waterproof material
15. stobs — O. purified by boiling and condensing the vapor
16. receded — P. device for collecting rainwater
17. cellophane — Q. embankments to prevent flooding
18. debris — R. something inherited
19. legacy — S. manage in doing something
20. scour — T. saying something softly

MULTIPLE CHOICE UNIT TEST 2 *The Cay*

I. Matching/Identify

Directions: Place the letter of the matching definition on the blank line.

_____ 1. Willemstad   A. city where the Enrights lived

_____ 2. Timothy   B. Dutch oil producing island

_____ 3. Devil's Mouth   C. Timothy's home

_____ 4. Curaçao   D. wanted to stay on the water

_____ 5. Phillip   E. thought the family should stay were they were

_____ 6. Charlotte Amalie   F. wanted to return to Norfolk

_____ 7. *SS Hato*   G. tanker torpedoed by the Germans

_____ 8. *SS Empire Tern*   H. had to be abandoned after being torpedoed

_____ 9. Mr. Enright   I. group of cays cut off by a coral reef

_____ 10. Mrs. Enright   J. wanted to head for land

II. Multiple Choice

1. What did Phillip do that he was not supposed to do?
    A. He skipped school.
    B. He went into Punda and Ft. Amsterdam with Henrik to see the U boats.
    C. He played with some of the native children.
    D. He listened to news of the war on the radio.

2. Phillip overheard his parents' conversation about his mother wanting to leave the island. What did Phillip do in response to what he overheard?
    A. He interrupted his parents and said he would not leave.
    B. He stayed awake most of the night.
    C. He wrote a letter to his parents and put it under their bedroom door.
    D. He ran to his friend Henrik's house and cried.

Multiple Choice Unit Test 2 *The Cay*

3. How did Phillip and his mother get separated after the *Hato* was torpedoed?
    A. The *Hato* lurched as they were getting into the lifeboat. The lifeboat tilted and the passengers landed in the water.
    B. Phillip ran back to the cabin to get something and was put in a different lifeboat.
    C. There was not enough room in the lifeboat for everyone so his mother put Phillip in and she stayed on the ship.
    D. Phillip's mother fainted on the deck of the Hato. The doctor kept her onboard to treat her. Then he put her in the lifeboat with him and the crew.

4. While on the raft, Timothy told Phillip they had something very important to do. What was it?
    A. stay alive
    B. get some sleep
    C. set up signal flares
    D. find land

5. What did Timothy say about Phillip's blindness?
    A. It was punishment because he was angry at his mother.
    B. It was not as bad as it could have been.
    C. It was terrible misfortune.
    D. It was natural and temporary.

6. Which statement is true?
    A. Both Phillip and Timothy wanted to get to land.
    B. Phillip wanted to get to land but Timothy wanted to stay on the raft.
    C. Phillip wanted to stay on the raft but Timothy wanted to get onto land.
    D. Both Phillip and Timothy wanted to stay on the raft.

7. What was Timothy worried about?
    A. He thought the island might be an ancient burial ground, which was good luck.
    B. He thought the island was unstable and might sink.
    C. He thought there might be pirates on the island.
    D. He thought the island might be hard to get to because of surrounding coral.

8. Phillip asked Timothy why there were different colors of skin. What was Timothy's answer?
    A. He said it was because the sun in some areas made people darker.
    B. He said he didn't know, but he believed all were the same under the skin.
    C. He said it was a curse put upon people by a devil.
    D. He said it was a challenge to make people work together.

Multiple Choice Unit Test 2 *The Cay*

9. Phillip knew that Timothy was trying to make him more independent in case ___.
    A. Timothy became too weak to work.
    B. Timothy lost his sight, too.
    C. Timothy died.
    D. Timothy got tired of doing all the work.

10. How does the story end?
    A. Timothy, Phillip, and Stew Cat are rescued. They all return to Willemstad. Phillip remains blind.
    B. Timothy dies after the hurricane. Phillip and Stew Cat are rescued. Phillip regains his sight after three operations.
    C. Timothy, Phillip, and Stew Cat are rescued. Timothy goes to Norfolk, Virginia with the Enright family. Phillip remains blind.
    D. Timothy and Phillip are rescued. Stew Cat dies before the rescue. Timothy goes back to Jamaica. Phillip returns to Willemstad.

III. Quotations
Identify the speaker:

          A. Phillip   C. Mrs. Enright   E. Mr. Enright
          B. Timothy   D. man from the rescue boat F. ship's captain

1. "I was not frightened, just terribly excited. War was something I'd heard a lot about, but had never seen."

2. "There's more danger in the trip back, unless you go by air, than there is in staying here. If they do shell us, they won't hit Scharloo."

3. "Do not be despair, young bahss. Someone will fin' us. Many schooner go by dis way, an' dis also be d'ship track to Jamaica, an' on."

4. "They are not the same as you, Phillip. They are different and they live differently. That's the way it must be."

5. "I want to be your friend."

6. "You see, Phill-eep, you do not need d'eye now. You 'ave done widout d'eye what I couldn't do wid my whole body."

The Cay Multiple Choice Unit Test 2 Quotations Continued

7. "Why didn't you take us with you?"

8. "Are you all right?"

9. "Son, get some sleep. The *Hato* was sunk way back in April."

10. "Phillip, I'm sorry, I'm so sorry."

IV. Vocabulary Matching

1. span
2. refinery
3. alabaster
4. ebony
5. cay
6. fronds
7. drone
8. awash
9. crevices
10. veils
11. eerie
12. welted
13. unraveled
14. groped
15. vanished
16. flailing
17. scour
18. stobs
19. malaria
20. navigation

A. small, low island
B. narrow cracks
C. stakes
D. low, humming sound
E. thrashing or moving around violently
F. extend over or across something
G. unnerving, suggesting a supernatural connection
H. having ridges or bumps on the skin
I. disappeared
J. took apart; unwound
K. searched by feeling
L. large, divided leaves
M. illness transmitted by mosquitoes
N. place for processing raw materials such as oil or sugar
O. search for something carefully
P. curtain-like things
Q. white mineral used for decorative plaster work
R. covered in water
S. directing a vehicle's course
T. brownish black color

ANSWER SHEET Multiple Choice Unit Tests *The Cay*

I. Matching

1. _____
2. _____
3. _____
4. _____
5. _____
6. _____
7. _____
8. _____
9. _____
10. _____

II. Multiple Choice

1. (A) (B) (C) (D)
2. (A) (B) (C) (D)
3. (A) (B) (C) (D)
4. (A) (B) (C) (D)
5. (A) (B) (C) (D)
6. (A) (B) (C) (D)
7. (A) (B) (C) (D)
8. (A) (B) (C) (D)
9. (A) (B) (C) (D)
10. (A) (B) (C) (D)

III. Quotations

1. _____
2. _____
3. _____
4. _____
5. _____
6. _____
7. _____
8. _____
9. _____
10. _____

IV. Vocabulary

1. _____
2. _____
3. _____
4. _____
5. _____
6. _____
7. _____
8. _____
9. _____
10. _____

Part 2

1. _____
2. _____
3. _____
4. _____
5. _____
6. _____
7. _____
8. _____
9. A
10. B

ANSWER SHEET KEY   Multiple Choice Unit Test 1 *The Cay*

I. Matching

1. J
2. E
3. H
4. I
5. B
6. G
7. A
8. C
9. D
10. F

II. Multiple Choice

1. (A) (B) (C) ( )
2. (A) (B) ( ) (D)
3. (A) ( ) (C) (D)
4. (A) ( ) (C) (D)
5. A) (B) ( ) (D)
6. ( ) (B) (C) (D)
7. ( ) (B) (C) (D)
8. ( ) (B) (C) (D)
9. (A) (B) (C) ( )
10. ( ) (B) (C) (D)

III. Quotations

1. D
2. B
3. E
4. A
5. E
6. F
7. C
8. A
9. A
10. C

IV. Vocabulary

1. D
2. K
3. Q
4. O
5. M
6. S
7. T
8. L
9. E
10. P
11. C
12. A
13. G
14. I
15. B
16. F
17. N
18. J
19. R
20. H

ANSWER SHEET KEY Multiple Choice Unit Test 2 *The Cay*

I. Matching
1. A
2. J
3. I
4. B
5. D
6. C
7. H
8. G
9. E
10. F

II. Multiple Choice
1. (A) (B) (C) ( )
2. (A) (B) ( ) (D)
3. (A) ( ) (C) (D)
4. (A) ( ) (C) (D)
5. A) (B) ( ) (D)
6. ( ) (B) (C) (D)
7. ( ) (B) (C) (D)
8. ( ) (B) (C) (D)
9. (A) (B) (C) ( )
10. ( ) (B) (C) (D)

III. Quotations
1. A
2. E
3. B
4. C
5. A
6. B
7. A
8. D
9. F
10. C

IV. Vocabulary
1. F
2. N
3. Q
4. T
5. A
6. L
7. D
8. R
9. PB
10. P
11. G
12. H
13. J
14. K
15. I
16. E
17. O
18. C
19. M
20. S

138

UNIT RESOURCES

BULLETIN BOARD IDEAS *The Cay*

1. Save one corner of the board for the best of students' *The Cay* writing assignments. You may want to use background maps the Caribbean area to represent the setting of the novel.

2. Take one of the word search puzzles from the extra activities packet and with a marker copy it over in a large size on the bulletin board. Write the clue words to find to one side. Invite students prior to and after class to find the words and circle them on the bulletin board.

3. Have students find or draw pictures that they think resemble the people and scenery in the book.

4. Invite students to help make an interactive bulletin board quiz. Give each student a half-sheet of paper (about 4"x5') folded in half so that it can open. On the outside flap, have each student write a description of one of the characters in the text. On the inside, they will write the name of the character. You can staple or tack these papers to the bulletin board so that the students can read the descriptions and lift the flaps to find the answers.

5. Collect and display pictures of the Caribbean islands.

6. Display articles about people who have survived alone or in groups after a shipwreck.

7. Display pictures and descriptions of U-boats, submarines, tankers, and freighters.

8. Display articles about Theodore Taylor.

9. Have students design postcards depicting the settings of the book.

10. Display a large map that includes the Caribbean Sea and islands, the east coast of the United States from Virginia to Florida, the Netherlands, and the Dutch West Indies. Have students locate the areas mentioned in the novel.

11. Display news clippings about World War II.

EXTRA ACTIVITIES PACKET *The Cay*

One of the difficulties in teaching a novel is that all students don't read at the same speed. One student who likes to read may take the book home and finish it in a day or two. Sometimes a few students finish the in-class assignments early. The problem, then, is finding suitable extra activities for students.

One thing that helps is to keep a little library in the classroom. For this unit on *The Cay* you might check out from the school or public library other books by Theodore Taylor. There are also many other survival and coming-of-age novels that students would enjoy reading. Magazines such as *Boy's Life* and *National Geographic World* contain articles about wilderness areas and young adults who do interesting things. Other related topics of interest might include any topics on the non-fiction assignment sheet, careers in the military or in the oil refinery or travel industries, travel books or magazines about the islands, etc.

Your students who have reading difficulties, or speak English as a second language may benefit from listening to all or part of the book on tape.

Other things you may keep on hand are word search puzzles. Several puzzles relating directly to *The Cay* are included in the unit. Feel free to duplicate them for your classroom use.

Some students may like to draw. You might devise a contest or allow some extra-credit grade for students who draw characters or scenes from *The Cay*. Note, too, that if the students do not want to keep their drawings you may pick up some extra bulletin board materials this way. If you have a contest and you supply the prize. You could, possibly, make the drawing itself a non-refundable entry fee. Take digital photos of the best projects and use them, enlarged, for a bulletin board, perhaps the next time you teach the unit.

Have maps, a globe, and travel brochures on hand for easy reference. Travel agencies and automobile clubs are good sources for these materials.

The pages which follow contain games, puzzles, and worksheets. The keys, when appropriate, immediately follow the puzzle or worksheet. Bingo cards immediately follow the bingo clues. There are two main groups of activities: one group for the unit; that is, generally relating to the *Cay* text, and another group of activities related strictly to the *Cay* vocabulary.

Directions for the games, puzzles, and worksheets are self-explanatory. The object here is to provide you with extra materials you may use in any way you choose.

MORE ACTIVITIES *The Cay*

1. Pick one of the incidents for students to dramatize. Encourage students to write dialog for the characters. (Perhaps you could assign various stories to different groups of students so more than one story could be acted and more students could participate.)

2. Have students design a bulletin board (ready to be put up; not just sketched) for *The Cay*.

3. Invite someone to talk to the class about survival after a shipwreck.

4. If you live near a military base, you may be able to have someone from the base come and talk about their survival training.

5. Ask someone from the Red Cross or the local paramedics to talk to the class about survival techniques.

6. Help students design and produce a talk show. Choose one of the story incidents as the topic. The host will interview the various characters. (Students should make up the questions they want the host to ask the characters.)

7. Have students work in pairs to create an interview with one of the characters. One student should be the interviewer and the other should be the interviewee. Students can work together to compose questions for the interviewer to ask. Each pair of students could present their interview to the class.

8. Invite students who have read other books by Theodore Taylor to present booktalks to the class.

9. Invite students who have read a biography of Theodore Taylor to tell the class about his life.

10. Use some of the related topics (noted earlier for an in-class library) as topics for research, reports, or written papers, or as topics for guest speakers.

11. Invite a storyteller to tell one or more stories related to *The Cay* to the class.

12. Invite someone who has lived in one of the areas mentioned in the book to speak to the class.

13. Have students hold small group discussions related to topics in the book. Assign a recorder and a speaker for each group. Have the speaker from each group make a report to the class.

14. Have students work in small groups to write a sequel telling what happened to Phillip after he returned from his ordeal.

15. Have students write a survival plan of their own. This could be based on any natural or man-made disaster.

16. Theodore Taylor wrote a sequel to *The Cay* called *Timothy of the Cay*. Have students read the book and report on it.

17. Research the West Indies dialect that Timothy spoke. (It is sometimes called the Calypso dialect.) Make a dictionary of words writtten in the dialect and in standard English.

18. Bring in calypso music and play it for the class.

19. Write additional chapters for the book, telling what Phillip's parents were doing during the time that he was on the island.

20. Write a chapter for the book describing the rescue of the rest of the people on the *Hato*.

21. Use the Internet to find out more about the island of Curaçao and the city of Willemstad. The teacher should preview any Web site before allowing students to access it. The following Web sites have information about Curaçao:
    - General History of Willemstad, World Heritage City
      http://www.geocities.com/willemstadorg/WstadHis/wstadhis.html
    - Historical Buildings in Scharloo
      http://www.curacao-diving.com/special/historic/Scharloo/Index.com

Word Litst The Cay

No.	Word	Clue/Definition
1.	AMERICAN	Nationality of Phillip and Timothy
2.	BAD	The cat was ___ luck.
3.	BAHSS	Timothy called Phillip Young ___.
4.	BELL	Sound that alerted Phillip his rescuers were coming
5.	BIRDS	They attacked Phillip.
6.	BLIND	Phillip lost his sight. He was ___.
7.	BRIDGE	Queen Emma was a ___
8.	CAN	They put a pebble in it each day.
9.	CONFLICT	Man vs. Nature, for example
10.	CORAL	It made navigating around the cays difficult.
11.	CURACAO	Place where Mr. Enright was sent to work
12.	DEVIL	___'s Mouth; name of the area of the cays
13.	ENRIGHT	Phillip's last name
14.	FISH	Phillip learned to do this to feed himself.
15.	GRAPE	Phillip used these oily leaves to make black smoke.
16.	HATO	Ship Phillip & his mother took towards Miami
17.	HELP	Word they spelled on the beach in stones
18.	HENRIK	Phillip's Dutch friend
19.	HUT	It was blown away.
20.	JULY	Month the hurricane hit
21.	JUMBI	Evil spirit
22.	KEG	They lashed the water ___ to a tree trunk.
23.	LANGOSTAS	Clawless lobsters Timothy caught for food
24.	MALARIA	Illness that struck Timothy
25.	MATS	Timothy asked Phillip to weave sleeping ___.
26.	MELON	Shape of the island
27.	MOTHER	I wouldn't even be here with you if it wasn't for my ___.
28.	NAZIS	They sent U-boats to destroy ships.
29.	PHILLIP	He regained his sight after operations.
30.	RAFT	It carried Timothy, Phillip & the cat
31.	REFINERY	Where Mr. Enright worked
32.	ROPE	Timothy made this with vines for Phillip.
33.	SEVENTY	Timothy was over ___ years old.
34.	SHARKS	Phillip fell off the raft into the water with ___.
35.	STEW	Name of the cook's cat
36.	SUN	Phillip covered Timothy in grape leaves to protect him from the ___.
37.	TANKERS	The Chinese crews on the ___ refused to sail.
38.	TAYLOR	Author Theodore
39.	TERN	After the sinking of the ___, Phillip began to understand that war meant death and destruction.
40.	THOMAS	Timothy's home was on St. ___
41.	TIMOTHY	Negro man who cared for Phillip
42.	TORPEDOED	The Hato was ___ on April 6, 1942.
43.	TREE	At first Phillip was too afraid to climb it.
44.	VIRGINIA	The Enrights were from this US state.
45.	WATER	Timothy & Phillip each had 1/2 cup of it to celebrate landfall.

WORD SEARCH - The Cay

```
S E V E N T Y P W T N M C O N F L I C T
D L L G K B L T H A B K O V D P N B P H
R H T D M E Y G A I T P K T K Z A M V W
I D Y I H P N D L N L E Y B H F C U T G
B V F R S S N V Q Z K L R A S E I J T D
D P V B R I G R M P R E I D N N R G N D
V F B S L H J T E N C C R P M D E X W W
R H J B F Z H T R F Y X N S H F M W L Z
Z D P Y R J B E X T I K B D B D A M P V
K V N Q T R T S P L Q N C W T Y S S V X
D K W X F X Y A R K G F E Y Q P Q G I P
B I X M G F D T T N P D Q R T C K H R K
W R X R S M J S T I H D E S Y O H K G X
J N N F A A T O F W M K H V P R P N I J
S E L T M T M G A G P O U G I A O B N C
G H A T O S E N R I G H T M A L A R I A
P S A P H R U A Q N S R A H E L C C A F
K H V R T S P L V I E K Y M Y E A F Z P
B W K Y K E C E F E X K L N V B R B L Y
N A Z I S S V A D M N E O Y J S U T L F
G F H J L Q G M N O P G R R Z T C U G F
Z C N S Q T F V D O E K F X G E J V B Q
T S Q P S B Q R R W Q D C G K W W J M D
```

AMERICAN	CORAL	HUT	NAZIS	TANKERS
BAD	CURACAO	JULY	PHILLIP	TAYLOR
BAHSS	DEVIL	JUMBI	RAFT	TERN
BELL	ENRIGHT	KEG	REFINERY	THOMAS
BIRDS	FISH	LANGOSTAS	ROPE	TIMOTHY
BLIND	GRAPE	MALARIA	SEVENTY	TORPEDOED
BRIDGE	HATO	MATS	SHARKS	TREE
CAN	HELP	MELON	STEW	VIRGINIA
CONFLICT	HENRIK	MOTHER	SUN	WATER

WORD SEARCH ANSWER KEY - The Cay

AMERICAN	CORAL	HUT	NAZIS	TANKERS
BAD	CURACAO	JULY	PHILLIP	TAYLOR
BAHSS	DEVIL	JUMBI	RAFT	TERN
BELL	ENRIGHT	KEG	REFINERY	THOMAS
BIRDS	FISH	LANGOSTAS	ROPE	TIMOTHY
BLIND	GRAPE	MALARIA	SEVENTY	TORPEDOED
BRIDGE	HATO	MATS	SHARKS	TREE
CAN	HELP	MELON	STEW	VIRGINIA
CONFLICT	HENRIK	MOTHER	SUN	WATER

CROSSWORD - The Cay

Across

1. Sound that alerted Phillip his rescuers were coming
5. Evil spirit
7. Phillip's last name
10. After the sinking of the ___, Phillip began to understand that war meant death and destruction.
11. Phillip learned to do this to feed himself.
14. Timothy called Phillip Young ___.
17. They lashed the water ___ to a tree trunk.
18. Timothy & Phillip each had 1/2 cup of it to celebrate landfall.
19. Phillip covered Timothy in grape leaves to protect him from the ___.
22. Shape of the island
24. It carried Timothy, Phillip & the cat
25. Nationality of Phillip and Timothy

Down

1. They attacked Phillip.
2. Clawless lobsters Timothy caught for food
3. Phillip lost his sight. He was ___.
4. It was blown away.
5. Month the hurricane hit
6. Illness that struck Timothy
8. Ship Phillip & his mother took towards Miami
9. Phillip used these oily leaves to make black smoke.
12. Man vs. Nature, for example
13. They put a pebble in it each day.
14. Queen Emma was a ____
15. Word they spelled on the beach in stones
16. Name of the cook's cat
20. Phillip's Dutch friend
21. Timothy asked Phillip to weave sleeping _____.
23. The cat was ___ luck.

CROSSWORD ANSWER KEY - The Cay

						¹B	E	²L	³B		⁴H		
		⁵J	U	⁶M	B	I		A	L		U		
		U		A		R	⁷E	N	R	I	⁸G	H	T
		L		L		D		G		N	H	A	⁹G
		Y		A		S		O		¹⁰D	T	E	R	N
				R		¹¹F	I	S	H		O		A
				I				T	¹²C		P
	¹³C		¹⁴B	A	¹⁵H	¹⁶S		A	O		¹⁷K	E	G
¹⁸W	A	T	E	R		E		T		¹⁹S	U	N	²⁰H
	N		I		L		E			F		E		²¹M
			D		P		²²W		M	E	L	O	N	A
		²³B		G						I		²⁴R	A	F	T
		²⁵A	M	E	R	I	C	A	N		C		I		S
		D									T		K	

Across
1. Sound that alerted Phillip his rescuers were coming
5. Evil spirit
7. Phillip's last name
10. After the sinking of the ___, Phillip began to understand that war meant death and destruction.
11. Phillip learned to do this to feed himself.
14. Timothy called Phillip Young ___.
17. They lashed the water ___ to a tree trunk.
18. Timothy & Phillip each had 1/2 cup of it to celebrate landfall.
19. Phillip covered Timothy in grape leaves to protect him from the ___.
22. Shape of the island
24. It carried Timothy, Phillip & the cat
25. Nationality of Phillip and Timothy

Down
1. They attacked Phillip.
2. Clawless lobsters Timothy caught for food
3. Phillip lost his sight. He was ___.
4. It was blown away.
5. Month the hurricane hit
6. Illness that struck Timothy
8. Ship Phillip & his mother took towards Miami
9. Phillip used these oily leaves to make black smoke.
12. Man vs. Nature, for example
13. They put a pebble in it each day.
14. Queen Emma was a ___
15. Word they spelled on the beach in stones
16. Name of the cook's cat
20. Phillip's Dutch friend
21. Timothy asked Phillip to weave sleeping _____.
23. The cat was ___ luck.

MATCHING 1 - The Cay

___ 1. TREE   A. Phillip lost his sight. He was ___.
___ 2. MATS   B. It was blown away.
___ 3. MELON   C. The Enrights were from this US state.
___ 4. BLIND   D. Month the hurricane hit
___ 5. JUMBI   E. Evil spirit
___ 6. GRAPE   F. Ship Phillip & his mother took towards Miami
___ 7. PHILLIP   G. ___'s Mouth; name of the area of the cays
___ 8. SUN   H. Timothy & Phillip each had 1/2 cup of it to celebrate landfall.
___ 9. REFINERY   I. Queen Emma was a ___
___ 10. DEVIL   J. Place where Mr. Enright was sent to work
___ 11. ENRIGHT   K. He regained his sight after operations.
___ 12. CURACAO   L. Timothy asked Phillip to weave sleeping ___.
___ 13. CONFLICT   M. At first Phillip was too afraid to climb it.
___ 14. CORAL   N. Timothy made this with vines for Phillip.
___ 15. HUT   O. The Chinese crews on the ___ refused to sail.
___ 16. BRIDGE   P. Man vs. Nature, for example
___ 17. JULY   Q. Phillip used these oily leaves to make black smoke.
___ 18. HENRIK   R. Phillip's Dutch friend
___ 19. WATER   S. It made navigating around the cays difficult.
___ 20. BAD   T. Phillip covered Timothy in grape leaves to protect him from the ___.
___ 21. VIRGINIA   U. Phillip's last name
___ 22. HATO   V. The cat was ___ luck.
___ 23. ROPE   W. Shape of the island
___ 24. FISH   X. Phillip learned to do this to feed himself.
___ 25. TANKERS   Y. Where Mr. Enright worked

MATCHING 1 ANSWER KEY - The Cay

M - 1. TREE	A.	Phillip lost his sight. He was ___.
L - 2. MATS	B.	It was blown away.
W - 3. MELON	C.	The Enrights were from this US state.
A - 4. BLIND	D.	Month the hurricane hit
E - 5. JUMBI	E.	Evil spirit
Q - 6. GRAPE	F.	Ship Phillip & his mother took towards Miami
K - 7. PHILLIP	G.	___'s Mouth; name of the area of the cays
T - 8. SUN	H.	Timothy & Phillip each had 1/2 cup of it to celebrate landfall.
Y - 9. REFINERY	I.	Queen Emma was a ___
G - 10. DEVIL	J.	Place where Mr. Enright was sent to work
U - 11. ENRIGHT	K.	He regained his sight after operations.
J - 12. CURACAO	L.	Timothy asked Phillip to weave sleeping ___.
P - 13. CONFLICT	M.	At first Phillip was too afraid to climb it.
S - 14. CORAL	N.	Timothy made this with vines for Phillip.
B - 15. HUT	O.	The Chinese crews on the ___ refused to sail.
I - 16. BRIDGE	P.	Man vs. Nature, for example
D - 17. JULY	Q.	Phillip used these oily leaves to make black smoke.
R - 18. HENRIK	R.	Phillip's Dutch friend
H - 19. WATER	S.	It made navigating around the cays difficult.
V - 20. BAD	T.	Phillip covered Timothy in grape leaves to protect him from the ___.
C - 21. VIRGINIA	U.	Phillip's last name
F - 22. HATO	V.	The cat was ___ luck.
N - 23. ROPE	W.	Shape of the island
X - 24. FISH	X.	Phillip learned to do this to feed himself.
O - 25. TANKERS	Y.	Where Mr. Enright worked

MATCHING 2 - The Cay Unit

___ 1. BIRDS   A. Month the hurricane hit
___ 2. SEVENTY   B. They lashed the water ___ to a tree trunk.
___ 3. CONFLICT   C. Phillip used these oily leaves to make black smoke.
___ 4. BLIND   D. Ship Phillip & his mother took towards Miami
___ 5. DEVIL   E. Timothy asked Phillip to weave sleeping _____.
___ 6. ROPE   F. Where Mr. Enright worked
___ 7. MOTHER   G. Negro man who cared for Phillip
___ 8. RAFT   H. Man vs. Nature, for example
___ 9. HATO   I. Timothy called Phillip Young ___.
___10. LANGOSTAS   J. I wouldn't even be here with you if it wasn't for my ____.
___11. TIMOTHY   K. Phillip lost his sight. He was ___.
___12. MELON   L. Timothy's home was on St. ____
___13. JUMBI   M. It made navigating around the cays difficult.
___14. CORAL   N. ____'s Mouth; name of the area of the cays
___15. FISH   O. The Enrights were from this US state.
___16. JULY   P. Evil spirit
___17. AMERICAN   Q. It carried Timothy, Phillip & the cat
___18. VIRGINIA   R. Phillip's Dutch friend
___19. KEG   S. Timothy was over ___ years old.
___20. BAHSS   T. They attacked Phillip.
___21. REFINERY   U. Timothy made this with vines for Phillip.
___22. MATS   V. Phillip learned to do this to feed himself.
___23. HENRIK   W. Nationality of Phillip and Timothy
___24. GRAPE   X. Shape of the island
___25. THOMAS   Y. Clawless lobsters Timothy caught for food

MATCHING 2 ANSWER KEY - The Cay Unit

T - 1.	BIRDS	A.	Month the hurricane hit
S - 2.	SEVENTY	B.	They lashed the water ___ to a tree trunk.
H - 3.	CONFLICT	C.	Phillip used these oily leaves to make black smoke.
K - 4.	BLIND	D.	Ship Phillip & his mother took towards Miami
N - 5.	DEVIL	E.	Timothy asked Phillip to weave sleeping _____.
U - 6.	ROPE	F.	Where Mr. Enright worked
J - 7.	MOTHER	G.	Negro man who cared for Phillip
Q - 8.	RAFT	H.	Man vs. Nature, for example
D - 9.	HATO	I.	Timothy called Phillip Young ___.
Y -10.	LANGOSTAS	J.	I wouldn't even be here with you if it wasn't for my ____.
G -11.	TIMOTHY	K.	Phillip lost his sight. He was ___.
X -12.	MELON	L.	Timothy's home was on St. ____
P -13.	JUMBI	M.	It made navigating around the cays difficult.
M -14.	CORAL	N.	____'s Mouth; name of the area of the cays
V -15.	FISH	O.	The Enrights were from this US state.
A -16.	JULY	P.	Evil spirit
W 17.	AMERICAN	Q.	It carried Timothy, Phillip & the cat
O -18.	VIRGINIA	R.	Phillip's Dutch friend
B -19.	KEG	S.	Timothy was over ___ years old.
I - 20.	BAHSS	T.	They attacked Phillip.
F -21.	REFINERY	U.	Timothy made this with vines for Phillip.
E -22.	MATS	V.	Phillip learned to do this to feed himself.
R -23.	HENRIK	W.	Nationality of Phillip and Timothy
C -24.	GRAPE	X.	Shape of the island
L -25.	THOMAS	Y.	Clawless lobsters Timothy caught for food

JUGGLE LETTERS 1 - The Cay

1. ETER = 1. _____
   At first Phillip was too afraid to climb it.

2. GIRVIIAN = 2. _____
   The Enrights were from this US state.

3. ACNMAREI = 3. _____
   Nationality of Phillip and Timothy

4. DLNIB = 4. _____
   Phillip lost his sight. He was ___.

5. ZANSI = 5. _____
   They sent U-boats to destroy ships.

6. TEWS = 6. _____
   Name of the cook's cat

7. ERTN = 7. _____
   After the sinking of the ___, Phillip began to understand that war meant death and destruction.

8. OHAT = 8. _____
   Ship Phillip & his mother took towards Miami

9. EOHMTR = 9. _____
   I wouldn't even be here with you if it wasn't for my ____.

10. BDA =10. _____
    The cat was ___ luck.

11. EODEPOTRD =11. _____
    The Hato was ___ on April 6, 1942.

12. ICFCNLOT =12. _____
    Man vs. Nature, for example

13. LJYU =13. _____
    Month the hurricane hit

14. RACLO =14. _____
    It made navigating around the cays difficult.

15. SDBIR =15. _____
They attacked Phillip.

16. TTOHYIM =16. _____
Negro man who cared for Phillip

17. EYRERIFN =17. _____
Where Mr. Enright worked

18. HAMOTS =18. _____
Timothy's home was on St. ____

19. EGK =19. _____
They lashed the water ___ to a tree trunk.

20. ASTAGOLSN =20. _____
Clawless lobsters Timothy caught for food

21. ASTERKN =21. _____
The Chinese crews on the ___ refused to sail.

22. AIMAARL =22. _____
Illness that struck Timothy

23. REIKHN =23. _____
Phillip's Dutch friend

JUGGLE LETTERS 1 ANSWER KEY - The Cay

1. ETER = 1. TREE
At first Phillip was too afraid to climb it.

2. GIRVIIAN = 2. VIRGINIA
The Enrights were from this US state.

3. ACNMAREI = 3. AMERICAN
Nationality of Phillip and Timothy

4. DLNIB = 4. BLIND
Phillip lost his sight. He was ___.

5. ZANSI = 5. NAZIS
They sent U-boats to destroy ships.

6. TEWS = 6. STEW
Name of the cook's cat

7. ERTN = 7. TERN
After the sinking of the ___, Phillip began to understand that war meant death and destruction.

8. OHAT = 8. HATO
Ship Phillip & his mother took towards Miami

9. EOHMTR = 9. MOTHER
I wouldn't even be here with you if it wasn't for my ___.

10. BDA = 10. BAD
The cat was ___ luck.

11. EODEPOTRD = 11. TORPEDOED
The Hato was ___ on April 6, 1942.

12. ICFCNLOT = 12. CONFLICT
Man vs. Nature, for example

13. LJYU = 13. JULY
Month the hurricane hit

14. RACLO = 14. CORAL
It made navigating around the cays difficult.

15. SDBIR   =15. BIRDS

                         They attacked Phillip.

16. TTOHYIM   =16. TIMOTHY

                         Negro man who cared for Phillip

17. EYRERIFN   =17. REFINERY

                         Where Mr. Enright worked

18. HAMOTS   =18. THOMAS

                         Timothy's home was on St. ____

19. EGK   =19. KEG

                         They lashed the water ____ to a tree trunk.

20. ASTAGOLSN   =20. LANGOSTAS

                         Clawless lobsters Timothy caught for food

21. ASTERKN   =21. TANKERS

                         The Chinese crews on the ____ refused to sail.

22. AIMAARL   =22. MALARIA

                         Illness that struck Timothy

23. REIKHN   =23. HENRIK

                         Phillip's Dutch friend

JUGGLE LETTERS 2 - The Cay

1. LBLE = 1. _____
   Sound that alerted Phillip his rescuers were coming

2. NAC = 2. _____
   They put a pebble in it each day.

3. NLEOM = 3. _____
   Shape of the island

4. HBASS = 4. _____
   Timothy called Phillip Young ___.

5. DEIRGB = 5. _____
   Queen Emma was a ____

6. SFIH = 6. _____
   Phillip learned to do this to feed himself.

7. AFTR = 7. _____
   It carried Timothy, Phillip & the cat

8. IVDEL = 8. _____
   ____'s Mouth; name of the area of the cays

9. KASSHR = 9. _____
   Phillip fell off the raft into the water with _____.

10. HNTIRGE =10. _____
    Phillip's last name

11. AMST =11. _____
    Timothy asked Phillip to weave sleeping _____.

12. PPHIILL =12. _____
    He regained his sight after operations.

13. VEEYNTS =13. _____
    Timothy was over ___ years old.

14. LPEH =14. _____
    Word they spelled on the beach in stones

15. TEWRA =15. _____
    Timothy & Phillip each had 1/2 cup of it to celebrate landfall.

16. UHT =16. _____
It was blown away.

17. UNS =17. _____
Phillip covered Timothy in grape leaves to protect him from the ____.

18. MUIBJ =18. _____
Evil spirit

19. PERO =19. _____
Timothy made this with vines for Phillip.

20. RAGEP =20. _____
Phillip used these oily leaves to make black smoke.

21. AROUCAC =21. _____
Place where Mr. Enright was sent to work

22. TARLOY =22. _____
Author Theodore

JUGGLE LETTERS 2 ANSWER KEY - The Cay

1. LBLE = 1. BELL
   Sound that alerted Phillip his rescuers were coming

2. NAC = 2. CAN
   They put a pebble in it each day.

3. NLEOM = 3. MELON
   Shape of the island

4. HBASS = 4. BAHSS
   Timothy called Phillip Young ___.

5. DEIRGB = 5. BRIDGE
   Queen Emma was a ___

6. SFIH = 6. FISH
   Phillip learned to do this to feed himself.

7. AFTR = 7. RAFT
   It carried Timothy, Phillip & the cat

8. IVDEL = 8. DEVIL
   ___'s Mouth; name of the area of the cays

9. KASSHR = 9. SHARKS
   Phillip fell off the raft into the water with ___.

10. HNTIRGE = 10. ENRIGHT
    Phillip's last name

11. AMST = 11. MATS
    Timothy asked Phillip to weave sleeping ___.

12. PPHIILL = 12. PHILLIP
    He regained his sight after operations.

13. VEEYNTS = 13. SEVENTY
    Timothy was over ___ years old.

14. LPEH = 14. HELP
    Word they spelled on the beach in stones

15. TEWRA = 15. WATER
    Timothy & Phillip each had 1/2 cup of it to celebrate landfall.

16. UHT =16. HUT
It was blown away.

17. UNS =17. SUN
Phillip covered Timothy in grape leaves to protect him from the ____.

18. MUIBJ =18. JUMBI
Evil spirit

19. PERO =19. ROPE
Timothy made this with vines for Phillip.

20. RAGEP =20. GRAPE
Phillip used these oily leaves to make black smoke.

21. AROUCAC =21. CURACAO
Place where Mr. Enright was sent to work

22. TARLOY =22 TAYLOR
Author Theodore

VOCABULARY RESOURCE MATERIALS

Vocabulary Word List The Cay

No.	Word	Clue/Definition
1.	ALABASTER	Type of gypsum (white mineral) usually used for decorative plaster work
2.	ANGUISH	Extreme anxiety
3.	AWASH	Covered in water
4.	CATCHMENT	Device for collecting rain water
5.	CAY	Small, low island
6.	CEASE	Stop
7.	CELLOPHANE	Thin, transparent, waterproof material made from wood pulp
8.	COARSER	Rougher
9.	CREVICES	Narrow cracks
10.	DEBRIS	Fragments of broken things
11.	DIKES	Embankments to prevent flooding
12.	DISTILLED	Purified by boiling and condensing vapors
13.	DRONE	Low, humming sound
14.	EBONY	Brownish-black color
15.	EERIE	Unnerving or unusual in a way that suggests a connection with the supernatural
16.	FARE	Manage in doing something
17.	FLAILING	Thrashing or moving violently or uncontrollably
18.	FRET	Worry
19.	FRONDS	Large, divided leaves
20.	GROPED	Searched by feeling
21.	HONING	Sharpening
22.	IDLING	Operating but not in gear
23.	IRRITATING	Annoying; bothersome
24.	LEEWARD	Away from the wind
25.	LEGACY	Something handed down or left via will
26.	MALARIA	Recurring illness common in hot countries, characterized by chills & fever
27.	MURMURING	Speaking softly
28.	MUTINY	Organized rebellion against ship's captain or another authority
29.	NAVIGATION	Directing a vehicle's course
30.	PARCH	Dry out
31.	RECEDED	Went back or further away
32.	REFINERY	Place for processing raw materials such as oil or sugar
33.	SCOUR	Search carefully
34.	SPAN	Extend over or across something
35.	STOBS	Stakes
36.	TETHERED	Tied to
37.	TREACHEROUS	Involving hidden dangers
38.	UNRAVELED	Took apart the strands of rope or yarn
39.	VANISHED	Disappeared
40.	VEILS	Like curtains
41.	WELTED	Having ridges or bumps on the skin caused by being struck with something (like a whip)
42.	WRENCHING	Pulling or twisting away

VOCABULARY WORD SEARCH - The Cay

```
T D H D W J A D C J Y Z Z H S W F E Y L
M H J I D Q N W H T F C N K T Q X E S E
L U Y Z D W G K G T K A E Q O Q D R L G
M A T L F L U N L N D A R A B T P I D A
C R D I S T I L L E D I K E S F R E T C
A G F P N R S N H M E R T E C E L G O Y
W X A R U Y H S G H B A V F B E R A N D
A N W M O R I S N C R L Y R V O R T A T
S L R Z P N E D I T I A K A P S N Y V W
H U D H A C D K T A S M R E E L T Y I N
M X V V I R D S A C L N D R A I R D G W
F B H V U E J X T Z U G E K L E E R A Q
Y X E O D F V C I V H V T C A V A O T N
D R C E Y I L W R C R J L D B V C N I J
C S C R K N D E R E H T E T A K H E O J
H E L J H E X A I E B N W V S T E P N J
R O V V Z R P F G Y N F K D T S R L N X
N V N W T Y Q H J W V C R N E L O Q J J
N R K I M Y T B L Q H A H B R R U F N S
T X T P N Q F T W K W Y L I W B S Q T P
T X T S Z G W N Y E Q J R Z N L W R T J
C K W L B S K Y E G D M J R N G K B B X
E N A H P O L L E C Z F L A I L I N G Q
```

ALABASTER	DEBRIS	FRONDS	MUTINY	TREACHEROUS
ANGUISH	DIKES	GROPED	NAVIGATION	UNRAVELED
AWASH	DISTILLED	HONING	PARCH	VANISHED
CATCHMENT	DRONE	IDLING	RECEDED	VEILS
CAY	EBONY	IRRITATING	REFINERY	WELTED
CEASE	EERIE	LEEWARD	SCOUR	WRENCHING
CELLOPHANE	FARE	LEGACY	SPAN	
COARSER	FLAILING	MALARIA	STOBS	
CREVICES	FRET	MURMURING	TETHERED	

VOCABULARY WORD SEARCH ANSWER KEY - The Cay

ALABASTER	DEBRIS	FRONDS	MUTINY	TREACHEROUS
ANGUISH	DIKES	GROPED	NAVIGATION	UNRAVELED
AWASH	DISTILLED	HONING	PARCH	VANISHED
CATCHMENT	DRONE	IDLING	RECEDED	VEILS
CAY	EBONY	IRRITATING	REFINERY	WELTED
CEASE	EERIE	LEEWARD	SCOUR	WRENCHING
CELLOPHANE	FARE	LEGACY	SPAN	
COARSER	FLAILING	MALARIA	STOBS	
CREVICES	FRET	MURMURING	TETHERED	

VOCABULARY CROSSWORD - The Cay

Across
1. Device for collecting rain water
6. Stakes
7. Thrashing or moving violently or uncontrollably
9. Unnerving or unusual in a way that suggests a connection with the supernatural
10. Search carefully
11. Extreme anxiety
14. Type of gypsum (white mineral) usually used for decorative plaster work
15. Embankments to prevent flooding
16. Sharpening
17. Like curtains

Down
2. Thin, transparent, waterproof material made from wood pulp
3. Tied to
4. Fragments of broken things
5. Small, low island
7. Manage in doing something
8. Directing a vehicle's course
10. Extend over or across something
11. Covered in water
12. Worry
13. Stop

VOCABULARY CROSSWORD ANSWER KEY - The Cay

					¹C	A	T	²C	H	M	E	³N	T	⁴D	
								E				E		E	
					⁵C		L			⁶S	T	O	B	S
				⁷F	L	A	I	L	⁸I	N	G		H		R
					A		Y		O		A	⁹E	E	R	I	E
	¹⁰S	C	O	U	R				P		V		R		S
	P			E					H		I		E		
	A								A		G		D		
¹¹A	N	G	U	I	S	H		N		A		¹²F		
W				¹³C		E		T		R			
¹⁴A	L	A	B	A	S	T	E	R		¹⁵D	I	K	E	S
S					A				O		T		
¹⁶H	O	N	I	N	G		S			N			
					¹⁷V	E	I	L	S				

Across
1. Device for collecting rain water
6. Stakes
7. Thrashing or moving violently or uncontrollably
9. Unnerving or unusual in a way that suggests a connection with the supernatural
10. Search carefully
11. Extreme anxiety
14. Type of gypsum (white mineral) usually used for decorative plaster work
15. Embankments to prevent flooding
16. Sharpening
17. Like curtains

Down
2. Thin, transparent, waterproof material made from wood pulp
3. Tied to
4. Fragments of broken things
5. Small, low island
7. Manage in doing something
8. Directing a vehicle's course
10. Extend over or across something
11. Covered in water
12. Worry
13. Stop

VOCABULARY MATCHING 1 - The Cay

___ 1. FLAILING   A. Directing a vehicle's course

___ 2. EBONY   B. Place for processing raw materials such as oil or sugar

___ 3. VEILS   C. Worry

___ 4. PARCH   D. Narrow cracks

___ 5. WELTED   E. Type of gypsum (white mineral) usually used for decorative plaster work

___ 6. CATCHMENT   F. Organized rebellion against ship's captain or another authority

___ 7. SPAN   G. Device for collecting rain water

___ 8. VANISHED   H. Thin, transparent, waterproof material made from wood pulp

___ 9. MURMURING   I. Small, low island

___10. ANGUISH   J. Dry out

___11. CAY   K. Like curtains

___12. IRRITATING   L. Thrashing or moving violently or uncontrollably

___13. DEBRIS   M. Extreme anxiety

___14. TREACHEROUS   N. Annoying; bothersome

___15. LEEWARD   O. Brownish-black color

___16. MUTINY   P. Fragments of broken things

___17. REFINERY   Q. Disappeared

___18. NAVIGATION   R. Extend over or across something

___19. ALABASTER   S. Having ridges or bumps on the skin caused by being struck with something (like a whip)

___20. CREVICES   T. Speaking softly

___21. RECEDED   U. Involving hidden dangers

___22. UNRAVELED   V. Away from the wind

___23. CELLOPHANE   W. Went back or further away

___24. COARSER   X. Rougher

___25. FRET   Y. Took apart the strands of rope or yarn

VOCABULARY MATCHING 1 ANSWER KEY - The Cay

L - 1. FLAILING	A.	Directing a vehicle's course
O - 2. EBONY	B.	Place for processing raw materials such as oil or sugar
K - 3. VEILS	C.	Worry
J - 4. PARCH	D.	Narrow cracks
S - 5. WELTED	E.	Type of gypsum (white mineral) usually used for decorative plaster work
G - 6. CATCHMENT	F.	Organized rebellion against ship's captain or another authority
R - 7. SPAN	G.	Device for collecting rain water
Q - 8. VANISHED	H.	Thin, transparent, waterproof material made from wood pulp
T - 9. MURMURING	I.	Small, low island
M -10. ANGUISH	J.	Dry out
I - 11. CAY	K.	Like curtains
N -12. IRRITATING	L.	Thrashing or moving violently or uncontrollably
P -13. DEBRIS	M.	Extreme anxiety
U -14. TREACHEROUS	N.	Annoying; bothersome
V -15. LEEWARD	O.	Brownish-black color
F -16. MUTINY	P.	Fragments of broken things
B -17. REFINERY	Q.	Disappeared
A -18. NAVIGATION	R.	Extend over or across something
E -19. ALABASTER	S.	Having ridges or bumps on the skin caused by being struck with something (like a whip)
D -20. CREVICES	T.	Speaking softly
W 21. RECEDED	U.	Involving hidden dangers
Y -22. UNRAVELED	V.	Away from the wind
H -23. CELLOPHANE	W.	Went back or further away
X -24. COARSER	X.	Rougher
C -25. FRET	Y.	Took apart the strands of rope or yarn

VOCABULARY MATCHING 2 - The Cay

___ 1. STOBS   A. Extreme anxiety

___ 2. FARE   B. Pulling or twisting away

___ 3. MALARIA   C. Organized rebellion against ship's captain or another authority

___ 4. EERIE   D. Stakes

___ 5. UNRAVELED   E. Took apart the strands of rope or yarn

___ 6. DIKES   F. Manage in doing something

___ 7. IDLING   G. Stop

___ 8. IRRITATING   H. Brownish-black color

___ 9. EBONY   I. Embankments to prevent flooding

___ 10. TREACHEROUS   J. Unnerving or unusual in a way that suggests a connection with the supernatural

___ 11. ALABASTER   K. Something handed down or left via will

___ 12. AWASH   L. Involving hidden dangers

___ 13. SPAN   M. Covered in water

___ 14. CREVICES   N. Annoying; bothersome

___ 15. CELLOPHANE   O. Narrow cracks

___ 16. NAVIGATION   P. Dry out

___ 17. DEBRIS   Q. Fragments of broken things

___ 18. MUTINY   R. Tied to

___ 19. PARCH   S. Recurring illness common in hot countries, characterized by chills & fever

___ 20. TETHERED   T. Like curtains

___ 21. ANGUISH   U. Thin, transparent, waterproof material made from wood pulp

___ 22. WRENCHING   V. Extend over or across something

___ 23. VEILS   W. Operating but not in gear

___ 24. CEASE   X. Type of gypsum (white mineral) usually used for decorative plaster work

___ 25. LEGACY   Y. Directing a vehicle's course

VOCABULARY MATCHING 2 ANSWER KEY - The Cay

D - 1.	STOBS	A.	Extreme anxiety
F - 2.	FARE	B.	Pulling or twisting away
S - 3.	MALARIA	C.	Organized rebellion against ship's captain or another authority
J - 4.	EERIE	D.	Stakes
E - 5.	UNRAVELED	E.	Took apart the strands of rope or yarn
I - 6.	DIKES	F.	Manage in doing something
W - 7.	IDLING	G.	Stop
N - 8.	IRRITATING	H.	Brownish-black color
H - 9.	EBONY	I.	Embankments to prevent flooding
L - 10.	TREACHEROUS	J.	Unnerving or unusual in a way that suggests a connection with the supernatural
X - 11.	ALABASTER	K.	Something handed down or left via will
M - 12.	AWASH	L.	Involving hidden dangers
V - 13.	SPAN	M.	Covered in water
O - 14.	CREVICES	N.	Annoying; bothersome
U - 15.	CELLOPHANE	O.	Narrow cracks
Y - 16.	NAVIGATION	P.	Dry out
Q - 17.	DEBRIS	Q.	Fragments of broken things
C - 18.	MUTINY	R.	Tied to
P - 19.	PARCH	S.	Recurring illness common in hot countries, characterized by chills & fever
R - 20.	TETHERED	T.	Like curtains
A - 21.	ANGUISH	U.	Thin, transparent, waterproof material made from wood pulp
B - 22.	WRENCHING	V.	Extend over or across something
T - 23.	VEILS	W.	Operating but not in gear
G - 24.	CEASE	X.	Type of gypsum (white mineral) usually used for decorative plaster work
K - 25.	LEGACY	Y.	Directing a vehicle's course

VOCABULARY JUGGLE LETTERS - The Cay

1. ARAILAM = 1. _____
   Recurring illness common in hot countries, characterized by chills & fever

2. NTAIIIRGRT = 2. _____
   Annoying; bothersome

3. DIINLG = 3. _____
   Operating but not in gear

4. YAC = 4. _____
   Small, low island

5. ILGFAINL = 5. _____
   Thrashing or moving violently or uncontrollably

6. RNOED = 6. _____
   Low, humming sound

7. YNEBO = 7. _____
   Brownish-black color

8. IGNOHN = 8. _____
   Sharpening

9. UORSC = 9. _____
   Search carefully

10. ECASE =10. _____
    Stop

11. GIWHNENCR =11. _____
    Pulling or twisting away

12. DDERECE =12. _____
    Went back or further away

13. YITUMN =13. _____
    Organized rebellion against ship's captain or another authority

14. SLIDELTDI =14. _____
    Purified by boiling and condensing vapors

15. OTSSB =15. _____
Stakes

16. RFTE =16. _____
Worry

17. RNMURMUIG =17. _____
Speaking softly

18. ANPS =18. _____
Extend over or across something

19. APRCH =19. _____
Dry out

20. SFONDR =20. _____
Large, divided leaves

21. CTNEAHCTM =21. _____
Device for collecting rain water

22. OGDRPE =22. _____
Searched by feeling

23. TELWED =23. _____
Having ridges or bumps on the skin caused by being struck with something (like a whip)

24. THEETRED =24. _____
Tied to

25. SEKID =25. _____
Embankments to prevent flooding

26. CALEYG =26. _____
Something handed down or left via will

27. YNERIREF =27. _____
Place for processing raw materials such as oil or sugar

28. EIBRDS =28. _____
Fragments of broken things

29. REUSTAECROH =29. _____
                    Involving hidden dangers

30. IHDENVSA   =30. _____
                    Disappeared

31. RFAE   =31. _____
                    Manage in doing something

32. EVRESICC   =32. _____
                    Narrow cracks

33. AAWSH   =33. _____
                    Covered in water

34. NLLOEPHCEA =34. _____
                    Thin, transparent, waterproof material made from wood pulp

35. IAIVTANGON =35. _____
                    Directing a vehicle's course

36. ARAALBEST   =36. _____
                    Type of gypsum (white mineral) usually used for decorative plaster work

37. VRAUENLED   =37 _____
                    Took apart the strands of rope or yarn

38. RELDWEA   =38. _____
                    Away from the wind

39. NSIAHGU   =39. _____
                    Extreme anxiety

40. EEERI   =40. _____
                    Unnerving or unusual in a way that suggests a connection with the supernatural

41. SLEVI   =41. _____
                    Like curtains

42. OARERCS   =42. _____
                    Rougher

VOCABULARY JUGGLE LETTERS ANSWER KEY - The Cay

1. ARAILAM = 1. MALARIA
Recurring illness common in hot countries, characterized by chills & fever

2. NTAIIIRGRT = 2. IRRITATING
Annoying; bothersome

3. DIINLG = 3. IDLING
Operating but not in gear

4. YAC = 4. CAY
Small, low island

5. ILGFAINL = 5. FLAILING
Thrashing or moving violently or uncontrollably

6. RNOED = 6. DRONE
Low, humming sound

7. YNEBO = 7. EBONY
Brownish-black color

8. IGNOHN = 8. HONING
Sharpening

9. UORSC = 9. SCOUR
Search carefully

10. ECASE = 10. CEASE
Stop

11. GIWHNENCR = 11. WRENCHING
Pulling or twisting away

12. DDERECE = 12. RECEDED
Went back or further away

13. YITUMN = 13. MUTINY
Organized rebellion against ship's captain or another authority

14. SLIDELTDI = 14. DISTILLED
Purified by boiling and condensing vapors

15. OTSSB =15. STOBS
Stakes

16. RFTE =16. FRET
Worry

17. RNMURMUIG =17. MURMURING
Speaking softly

18. ANPS =18. SPAN
Extend over or across something

19. APRCH =19. PARCH
Dry out

20. SFONDR =20. FRONDS
Large, divided leaves

21. CTNEAHCTM =21. CATCHMENT
Device for collecting rain water

22. OGDRPE =22. GROPED
Searched by feeling

23. TELWED =23. WELTED
Having ridges or bumps on the skin caused by being struck with something (like a whip)

24. THEETRED =24. TETHERED
Tied to

25. SEKID =25. DIKES
Embankments to prevent flooding

26. CALEYG =26. LEGACY
Something handed down or left via will

27. YNERIREF =27. REFINERY
Place for processing raw materials such as oil or sugar

28. EIBRDS =28. DEBRIS
Fragments of broken things

29. REUSTAECROH =29. TREACHEROUS
Involving hidden dangers

30. IHDENVSA =30. VANISHED
Disappeared

31. RFAE =31. FARE
Manage in doing something

32. EVRESICC =32. CREVICES
Narrow cracks

33. AAWSH =33. AWASH
Covered in water

34. NLLOEPHCEA =34. CELLOPHANE
Thin, transparent, waterproof material made from wood pulp

35. IAIVTANGON =35. NAVIGATION
Directing a vehicle's course

36. ARAALBEST =36. ALABASTER
Type of gypsum (white mineral) usually used for decorative plaster work

37 VRAUENLED =37. UNRAVELED
Took apart the strands of rope or yarn

38. RELDWEA =38. LEEWARD
Away from the wind

39. NSIAHGU =39. ANGUISH
Extreme anxiety

40. EEERI =40. EERIE
Unnerving or unusual in a way that suggests a connection with the supernatural

41. SLEVI =41. VEILS
Like curtains

42. OARERCS =42. COARSER
Rougher

www.ingramcontent.com/pod-product-compliance
Lightning Source LLC
LaVergne TN
LVHW081534060526
838200LV00048B/2079